C000216518

Workplace Mediation Skills

Training Handbook

Clive Lewis OBE DL FCIPD

Published by Globis Ltd

1 Wheatstone Court, Waterwells Business Park

Quedgeley, Gloucester, GL2 2AQ

First published in Great Britain in 2012. Reprinted in 2014.

ISBN 978-0-9568648-7-1

Cover design by Brendan Vaughan-Spruce

Printed and bound in the UK by

Berforts Information Press

23-25 Gunnels Wood Park

Stevenage

Hertfordshire

SG1 2BH

Also by the author

Author's note

Welcome to the Globis Mediation Group Workplace Mediation Skills Training Handbook.

This guide is designed to accompany and complement the Globis National Employment and Workplace Mediation Certificate five day course. It contains information that will help you prepare for the course and give further help in your development as a workplace mediator. On the course you will have ample opportunity to practise the skills outlined in this handbook.

By training as an employment and workplace mediator, you are joining a small, but growing number of people in the UK who are developing skills in this important area.

We hope that you will find this handbook and the accompanying course both stimulating and rewarding. If you wish to learn more about Globis Mediation Group and how we help companies build better relationships at work, please contact us or visit www.globis.co.uk

May I wish you every success with your mediation career.

Clive Lewis OBE DL FCIPD
Managing Director
Globis Mediation Group

CONTENTS

The Background of Dispute Resolution

The Historical Context

Mediation is a derivative of the term 'Alternative Dispute Resolution' (ADR) which has its origins in the USA. ADR was introduced as an alternative to the legal system of dealing with disputes which was seen to be costly, adversarial, damaging to relationships and limited to rights-based remedies compared to creative problem solving. Since its emergence in the late 1970s, ADR has found a sympathetic audience amongst litigators and litigation users in many countries. The acceptance of the term ADR grew as the preferred term in the worlds of business and civil litigation.

Despite many lawyers training to become commercial mediators, there is varied acceptance in the legal profession to the concept of ADR – specifically mediation. With the emergence of workplace mediation, the primary embracers of the model are employment lawyers and HR professionals.

The strength of mediation lies in its flexibility of practice, where it has helped to introduce new ways of thinking and surface options available to parties engaged in a dispute or potential dispute. Mediation has introduced new thinking when it comes to moving from conflict to resolution. Of the many forms of alternative dispute resolution, mediation has proved to be the most flexible and user-friendly approach. Some countries, such as Australia and New Zealand, have been practising a form of mediation for many years.

In a commercial context, pressure is being put on the established courts to adopt mediation. The court's inability to deal with increasing caseloads is one of the reasons why the level of its adoption in the UK is increasing.

ADR began in earnest in the UK in 1990 and was established in three main fields. These were:

- Commercial
- Family
- Community

The need for mediation in the workplace is a nationwide issue. Few organisations are without problems in their established ways of working. The increase in the type and complexity of employment legislation since the early 1990's has had a major impact on HR professionals and line managers to manage people and introduce change. Today, employees generally have less loyalty to organisations, are well informed of both their statutory and human rights and are more willing to invoke them at the earliest opportunity.

One of the solutions available to organisations is mediation. Mediation is a voluntary, non-binding and "without prejudice" process in which a specially trained third party intervenes in a dispute and attempts to bring the parties together and agree a settlement. If the mediation succeeds, and over 90% of them do, then it ends with a binding agreement. If anyone is dissatisfied with the process, either party or the mediator may terminate the mediation at any time. The aggrieved individual may then proceed to assert their legal rights through the tribunal or court system.

Other forms of dispute resolution include negotiation, collaborative law, arbitration and early neutral evaluation.

The Legal Framework

Since the early 1990s numerous pieces of employment legislation have been imposed on UK organisations. These included changes such as:

- maternity and paternity provisions
- age discrimination
- equal pay monitoring
- protection for part time workers
- sexual orientation legislation
- religious belief legislation
- harassment and bullying discrimination legislation

The latest piece of legislation to have a substantial impact has been The Equality Act. In October 2010, The Equality Act became law in the UK. The Act has been designed to ensure that everybody is adequately protected against discrimination and emphasises a socio-economic duty to reduce inequality.

The Act has consolidated existing legislation on sex, race, disability, sexual orientation, religion or belief and age. If not followed or prepared for properly, it could result in significant costs for organisations. The Equalities Office is estimating that its implementation is likely to cost somewhere in the region of £310 million - mainly as a result of extra tribunal and court cases.

The Confederation of British Industry (CBI) regularly lobbies government on the cost of 'bureaucracy' being introduced to the UK. Latest estimates suggest this cost is as high as £40 billion per annum.

The effect of legislation introduced since the 1990s is colossal. HR professionals and line managers were spending large amounts of time ensuring that correct procedures were being followed when any indication of grievance or disciplinary measures were encountered. As a result, the number of grievance cases lodged with employment panels rose by a third during 2005/6. This was after claims initially fell by one quarter after the 2004 dispute resolution rules came in.

According to research by the Chartered Institute of Personnel and Development (CIPD), 29% of employers felt disputes were less likely to be resolved informally following the 2004 introduction of the statutory dispute resolution procedures.

The government asked Michael Gibbons to review the options for simplifying and improving all aspects of employment dispute resolution to make the system work better for both employers and employees. The review involved business representatives, unions and other interested parties in considering the options for change. Globis Mediation Group was one of the organisations which advised the Department for Business, Innovation and Skills (BIS) on the review.

BIS had gathered evidence about the effect of previous changes to the dispute resolution system. The review looked at all aspects of the system, including the current legal requirements, how employment tribunals work and the scope for new initiatives to help resolve disputes at an earlier stage.

In its document – *The Government of Britain* – the government's draft legislative programme, HM government planned to simplify the current employment regime.

New ACAS Code of Practice

The dispute resolution system costs the government around £120 million per year. The statutory procedures for handling discipline and grievance issues introduced in October 2004 were widely criticised for creating high administrative burdens and leading to the formalisation of disputes and for lawyers to become involved at an early stage. Although the provisions were only in force for less than five years, the statutory dispute resolution procedures were repealed when the provisions of the Employment Act 2008 were implemented.

The new ACAS code came into force on April 6th 2009 as part of the Employment Act 2008. This code is designed to help employers, employees and their representatives deal with disciplinary and grievance situations in the workplace more effectively. The concept of mediation was introduced within the code for the first time.

Employers and employees should always seek to resolve disciplinary and grievance issues in the workplace. Many potential disciplinary or grievance issues can be resolved informally. A quiet word is often all that is required to resolve an issue. Where this is not possible, employers and employees are increasingly using an independent third party to help resolve the problem. The third party need not come from outside the organisation, but could be an internal mediator, so long as they are not involved in the disciplinary or grievance issue. In some cases, an external mediator might be more appropriate.

The Business Case

Before going into the concept of mediation in any detail, it is important to lay a foundation that outlines the importance of mediation for today's organisations. The business case for early resolution is persuasive and is becoming underpinned by more and more evidence. Disputes at work cost money through lost management time, lower productivity, higher sickness and absenteeism and higher employee turnover. Research from the CIPD indicates that the annual cost of conflict at work to the UK economy is at least £24 billion. This is costly, particularly during a time of economic uncertainty. In some cases, line managers are spending about 24% of their time managing issues associated with conflict. Some of the other impacts of conflict in the workplace include:

- Reduced employee engagement
- Less likelihood of projects being delivered on time and on budget
- Increased theft and sabotage
- Lower employee attraction
- Potential interruptions to the supply chain
- Poor customer service delivery

Conflict in the workplace is a reality; anecdotal evidence suggests it may be increasing. The CIPD survey *Managing Conflict at Work* found that the main causes of conflict in order of importance were:

- Behaviour/conduct
- Performance
- Sickness absence
- Attendance
- Relationships between colleagues
- Theft/fraud
- Bullying/harassment
- Sex discrimination

Henry David Thoreau once said "the price of anything is the amount of life you pay for it". The topic of conflict resolution has a strong economic imperative. Conflict costs money. Costs might be seen through the impact on management time, poor health, a breakdown in customer relationships leading to a loss in revenue, or projects running over time and budget.

Over the last 15-20 years there have been a number of areas providing opportunities to achieve cost savings and competitive advantage that have captured the attention of business leaders. Conflict management perhaps represents the biggest unrecognised opportunity for cost reduction in today's workplace. In a time of economic uncertainty organisations often begin to look for new opportunities for efficiency. The strategic management of conflict represents a major opportunity for this.

A survey conducted several years ago by the American Management Association, responded to by 116 chief executive officers, 76 vice presidents and 66 middle managers, indicated that these managers spent 24% of their time resolving conflicts. If this example is applied to the UK, and it is assumed that on average the sample of managers earn a basic annual salary of £70,000, this equates to in excess of £4 million per year. There are, of course, many additional costs outside of basic salary, such as lost revenue, lost bonus, employee turnover, management time, impact on customer service and so on. Whichever way the maths is done, conflict is expensive.

There are examples of organisations which have realised significant cost savings by the strategic management of conflict resolution. Most data on this topic is US based, but it transfers well and is worth noting. Karl Slaikeu and Ralph Hasson in *Controlling the Costs of Conflict* list the following examples:

- In the first year of comparison, Brown and Root reported an 80% reduction in outside litigation expenses by introducing a systematic approach to collaboration and conflict resolution regarding employment issues.

- Motorola Corporation reported a reduction in outside litigation expenses of up to 75% per year over six years by using a systematic approach to conflict management in its legal department and including a mediation clause in its contracts with suppliers.

- National Cash Register Corporation reported a reduction in outside litigation expenses of 50% and a drop in its number of pending lawsuits from 263 to 28 following the systematic use of alternative dispute resolution.

- The US Air Force reported that by taking a collaborative approach to conflict management in a construction project, it completed the project 144 days ahead of schedule and $12 million under budget.

In another study of 1,600 employees it was found that:

- 22% of employees said that they had actually decreased their work efforts as a result of conflict.

- Over 50% reported that they lost work time because they worried about whether the instigator of the conflict would do it again.

- 12% reported that they had changed jobs in order to get away from the instigator.

At the University of Cologne, Andreas Brinkhoff and Ulrich Thonemann have researched supply chains for three years and found that the majority achieve less than expected. Almost all firms conduct joint projects with other firms, yet their study has shown that over 50% of supply chain management projects fail. They investigated 87 supply chain projects in the manufacturing and consumer industries to determine which factors led to either success or failure. They concentrated on inter-organisational initiatives, which are becoming increasingly more important in the current business environment.

The investigation revealed ten key problem areas (see below). The top five are decisive and by far the main causes of failure. Approximately 88% of successful supply chains were those which managed to avoid the five key problems.

1.	Objectives not clearly defined or agreed on
2.	Participating employees not committed to project
3.	Inadequate top management support
4.	Insufficient trust between partners
5.	Project leader lacks integrative skills
6.	Problems dealt with too slowly
7.	Progress not consistent
8.	Too little communication with partners
9.	Weak teams
10.	Conflicts with partners not solved constructively

These ten problem areas highlight the growing need for the business case to be explored further.

Globis Mediation Group was invited to help a department of 30 people rebuild relationships following a lengthy period of turbulence within the team. Over a six month period, the organisation was able to report a 93% reduction in sickness absence and a 60% reduction in labour turnover and associated costs. The reductions were calculated at an annual value of £143,000. This figure just scratches the surface. Globis Mediation Group predicted that if this type of scenario was being repeated in five other departments of 30 people across the organisation (one department for every one directorate and 1% of the workforce) the total annual cost saving would be in the region of £1 million. In reality the 1% figure is likely to be much higher. At a more realistic 10%, it would bring the cost savings figure to £8.5 million.

Globis Mediation Group worked with the management team to build a framework for a forum for debate, discussion, questioning, raising awareness of objectives and building relationships.

Mediation fits with a number of strategic initiatives that focus on building relationships in the workplace. Four of these initiatives are listed below:

Dame Carol Black Review

On average, UK workers are spending more time at work than a decade ago. One of the implications of this is that stress-related problems affecting morale and well-being continue to grow. The CBI suggests 175 million working days were lost to illness in 2006. It has been proven that a correlation exists between conflict and poor health. In some cases this can be chronic; in others it might be minor. A percentage of the 175 million days lost due to sickness will be as a result of employees staying away from work to avoid their opponent. Although the government commissioned 'Working for a Healthier Tomorrow' the report authored by Dame Carol Black doesn't make a direct correlation with the impact of conflict on health. It is proposed that mediation could be incorporated into the recommendations of this report to help reduce the £100 billion annual cost of sickness to the UK working population.

Boorman Review

A follow on from the 'Working for a Healthier Tomorrow' report has been the Boorman Review. A review of the health and well-being of NHS staff has found high levels of sickness and absence and is calling for a major restructure of systems to deal with the problems. The NHS Health and Well-being Review found that on average, NHS staff take 10.7 sick days per year compared to 9.7 days being taken across the public sector as a whole and 6.4 days for the private sector. The cost associated to these absences is in the region of £1.7 billion per year. The review found that absence in the NHS is reducing at a slower rate than in other parts of the public sector or in the private sector.

The report was led by Dr. Steve Boorman, chief medical advisor to the Royal Mail Group. He found incidents where staff continue to go to work when they are not fully fit or highly stressed. Staff also did not believe that line managers showed a positive interest in their health and well-being. The NHS Health and Well-being Review makes a number of recommendations and says that improvements could save the NHS more than £555 million a year and improve patient care.

Key recommendations include:

- Inclusion of staff health and well-being measures and performance monitoring in the NHS governance frameworks
- Publication and monitoring of key health and well-being statistics, including annual data on sickness absence
- A national minimum standard of OH (Occupational Health) services across the NHS
- An improved provision of wellness and early intervention services for staff

It is proposed that the role of mediation should be featured in order to help address absence problems in the NHS.

McLeod Review on Employee Engagement

David MacLeod and Nita Clarke were commissioned by BIS to take an in-depth look at employee engagement and to report on its potential benefits for organisations and employees. The then Secretary of State for Business, Lord Mandelson, encouraged the independent reviewers to examine whether a wider take up of engagement approaches could impact positively on UK competitiveness and performance and help meet the challenges of increased global competition.

Since autumn 2008, they have seen many examples, within companies and organisations, where performance and profitability have been transformed by employee engagement. They have met many employees who are only too keen to explain how their working lives have been transformed and have read many studies which show a clear correlation between engagement and performance – and most importantly between improving engagement and improving performance.

The report argues that wider delivery of employee engagement could have a positive impact on UK competitiveness and performance both during the downturn and in powering through to recovery. It concludes that while there are some excellent examples of good employee engagement, there are barriers to uptake, particularly amongst smaller businesses, and that government can play a unique role in giving the subject profile, and bringing together role models with those who have delivery mechanisms and levers to help galvanise the collective effort.

As change continues to be a constant, all companies will need to address the structures that keep the organisation on its feet. Ken Cloke refers to the sounds that are made by the cracks in organisational systems. The challenge to line managers and HR professionals is to hear these cracks as they develop and not to have selective hearing or become tone deaf with the application of appropriate solutions. For example, an organisation may be aware of a department leader who may cause relationship breakdowns amongst some colleagues. The response the organisation may pursue is to undertake an organisational restructure to try and fix the problem. Whilst this might address the issue of personality clashes, a bigger problem may emerge. This could be that the organisation now has a weaker structure to deliver against its corporate objectives. The perpetrator may also leave after some time, exposing the weakness in the misguided organisation structure. Although sometimes harder, it is always better to concentrate on the primary needs of the organisation rather than fit personalities into boxes. It may take time, money, energy and effort to resolve conflicts, but it takes much more time, money, energy and effort not to resolve them.

In a period where organisations are thinking of creative ways to save money, commissioning conflict resolution and mediation is a great investment.

The table below highlights the areas that are impacted when conflict exists:

Conflict Impact Areas	
Increases	Decreases
Customer complaints Employee turnover Sickness Absence Legal fees	Productivity Project delivery Employee attraction Well-being

For many employers, the business case will be founded largely on the cost of dealing with tribunal claims. The 2007 CIPD survey *Managing Conflict at Work* found that the average annual costs to employers of dealing with ET claims (excluding management time) was almost £20,000.

But management time is highly significant: businesses spend almost ten days on average dealing with an individual claim (including almost eight days of senior managers' time). 33% of employers also report non-financial negative effects.

Time - mediation is often completed in one meeting, compared with the two days or more typically required for tribunal hearings.

Resolving Workplace Disputes: Government response to the consultation - 2011
In November 2011 the Government released its response to the 'Resolving Workplace Disputes' consultation paper that had been circulated earlier that year.

In its response, the government outlined that their vision is for an employment dispute resolution system that promotes the use of early dispute resolution as a means of dealing with workplace problems.

The consultation "Resolving Workplace Disputes" set out these ideas and focuses on the need to tackle problems early, before they get to the tribunal stage. The government recognised that the system is not working as originally intended and is often not a positive experience for either employer or employee.

Consultation findings

Mediation: The government explored with large businesses within the retail sector whether and how they might be able to share their mediation expertise with smaller businesses in their supply chain, and piloted the creation of regional mediation networks through the provision of mediation training to a number of representatives from local SMEs.

Compromise Agreements: The government:

• Brought forward an amendment to clarify s.147 of the Equality Act, to provide reassurance to parties that compromise agreements can safely be used;

• Considered how it could develop a standard text for compromise agreements;

• Consulted on amending section 203(3)(b) of the Employment Rights Act 1996 to enable compromise agreements to cover existing and future claims without requiring long lists of causes of action;

• Consulted on introducing a system of "protected conversations";

• Amended the title of "compromise agreements" to "settlement agreements".

Financial Penalties: The government introduced a discretionary power for employment tribunals to levy a financial penalty on employers found to have breached employment rights.

Formula for calculating award and payment limits: The government retained the automatic mechanism for up-rating tribunal awards and statutory redundancy payments, but modified the formula to round to the nearest pound.

Employment tribunal review

In response to the Resolving Workplace Disputes consultation exercise, the government invited Mr Justice Underhill to review the employment tribunal system. Many stakeholders from the judiciary, the legal profession and business believed that the rules had become inflexible, unduly prescriptive and weren't conducive to effective case management. Mr Justice Underhill's recommendations are outlined below:

- Introduce a number of new rules to ensure effective case management, such as simplified and streamlined procedures for preliminary hearings and withdrawing cases

- Introduce new Presidential guidance which will provide all parties a better idea of what to expect and what will be expected of them at tribunal

- Introduce a stand-alone rule that gives employment tribunals and judges a clear mandate to encourage and facilitate the use of alternative forms of dispute resolution at all appropriate stages of the tribunal process

The Ministry of Justice also conducted a review of employment tribunal fees which ran as a separate piece of work to the above. Following this review, in the summer of 2013 fees for bringing a tribunal claim were introduced. One of the main aims of the introduction of fees was to encourage parties to consider other ways of resolving their disputes. Two levels of fees were introduced, type A for cases such as unpaid wages and redundancy payments, and type B for cases including discrimination complaints and unfair dismissal. Since the introduction of the fees, statistics published by the Ministry of Justice reveal a 79% drop in the number of cases between October and December 2013 compared to the previous year. UNISON have challenged the government's decision to introduce fees stating that the fees bar access to justice. The response from the High Court being that the system needs more time to show its impact before a decision can be made and this topic should be kept under government review.

Early conciliation

As part of the Enterprise and Regulatory Reform Act 2013, early conciliation was introduced from April 2014. The early conciliation scheme is run by Acas and has been introduced to reduce the number of claims going through to tribunal. Then key points are as follows:

- From 6th May 2014 it is a legal requirement (save exceptional circumstances) that anyone wishing to bring an employment tribunal must notify Acas.
- The claimant will be offered the free service of early conciliation as an opportunity to avoid the stress and cost of a tribunal.
- If the claimant is happy to proceed, Acas will then make reasonable attempts to contact the employer and facilitate early conciliation with the aim of reaching a settlement. The timescale allowed for early conciliation is four weeks with an additional 14 days available if required.
- If early conciliation is not successful, or one/both party is unwilling to participate, then a conciliation certificate will be issued, and an employment tribunal claim can be lodged.
- Once the early conciliation process has started, the time limits for bringing a tribunal claim are paused whilst the process is attempted. It is the claimant's responsibility to ensure that any claim is presented in time.

The first month of the service saw 4000 people contacting Acas, 98% going through to utilise early conciliation and the first case being settled within 24 hours. The scheme has got off to a successful start and we wait with interest to see how the scheme impacts on dispute resolution.

The Changing Environment of the Workplace

Today's world of work is almost unrecognisable from the workplace of only a few years ago. Employers and employees have no choice but to embrace revolutionary communication advances, the introduction of flexible working arrangements, greater diversity, organisational restructuring, outsourcing and off-shoring. The information age will continue to speed up the pace of change which organisations will need to adopt, or be faced with extinction.

Warren Bennis states 'as change is now constant in the workplace, the conflicts that inevitably accompany it can be seen everywhere. These conflicts sometimes create a crisis of leadership that has been reflected in the spate of corporate scandals that have unfolded before us'. As a result, CEOs appointed after 1990 are three times more likely to be sacked than CEOs appointed before that date.

The growing mistrust of business and government, together with concerns about the global economy, the aftermath of wars and increasingly fierce competition, are signs that corporate leaders are in need of help in both the prevention and resolution of conflict in the workplace.

Our relationships at work are generally based on three things: power, rights and interests. A line manager has the power to take actions and make decisions within their frame of reference, without consultation on a daily basis. We all have contractual, statutory and human rights that should be acknowledged and respected. It is, however, only when we consider the interests of each other that we are likely to get true value, satisfaction and a win-win outcome from our working relationships. Smart managers avoid the first two and focus on leading a team through the third.

The law is based on a mental level, while humans interact on an emotional level. The increasing levels and complexities of law at work are resulting in people finding it more restrictive to express emotions across a range of areas. This means that feelings become suppressed and when employees are unable to find an appropriate emotional channel through which to vent their feelings, they are left with few choices.

These choices may be:

1. Leave the organisation
2. Retaliate in some way
3. Complain to a higher authority or HR
4. Invoke the disciplinary and grievance procedures

Points 1, 2 and 4 are unlikely to result in resolution and closure of conflict. Point 3 may be beneficial if the line manager is competent in handling discussions of a confrontational nature. Recent research has shown, however, that few managers (37%) feel adequately trained to cope with conflict in the workplace.

Globis Mediation Group believes that not all problems should be laid at the door of the organisation. It is wrong to assume that a manager is responsible for keeping all employees happy. Some problems can be resolved on a personal basis. Some problems could even be beneficial to the work environment.

A change in the philosophy of leadership that encourages honesty of expression of conflict and promotes open discussion of differences is needed. This is likely to include a new concept of value; based on humanistic and democratic ideals which will replace depersonalised, bureaucratic-value systems that regard property and machines to be more important than people and relationships. Successful leaders value honest communications over power and bureaucracy. An organisation will have difficulty in being honest with its shareholders and the public if it is not honest with itself. Developing cultures of honesty in which conflict can be addressed is an ongoing effort that requires attention and guidance from the most senior levels in an organisation.

About Conflict

Over time, we all experience conflicts. Generally, these conflicts are based on miscommunication, misunderstanding, cultural differences, choice of language, poor leadership, ineffective management styles, unclear roles and responsibilities, differences in standards or fluctuating economic conditions.

Others may be based on cultural or gender differences, marital difficulties, family problems, abrasive or submissive personalities, insensitivity to feelings, personal disappointments, unmet needs, and a thousand other causes and factors which may have no direct correlation to our work or our goals and purposes in life.

These conflicts can have a big impact on our places of work. They can reduce productivity and morale, occupy a great deal of conscious and unconscious attention, create problems for HR and staff and lead, if uncorrected, to litigation, bitterness, poor morale, wasted time and resources, rumours, employee turnover and reduced opportunities for change.

Additionally, many of the conflicts in our lives that are sorted out do not reach the attitudes and emotions that, if left unresolved, only emerge later to create new future problems.

It has been estimated that 90% of health problems can be prevented or managed by wise choices that we make about our own health, such as eating a balanced diet, exercising regularly, maintaining positive social and family relationships, avoiding smoking and excessive alcohol etc. By making wise choices about how we handle conflicts, especially before they escalate and become crises, we can also prevent or manage an equal percentage of conflicts.

In March 2008, the CBI reported that sick leave was costing the UK economy around £1.6 billion per year. Those surveyed said they believed that 12% of days taken off by workers were not genuine.

Overall workplace absence, including genuine illness, cost the economy about £13.4 billion in 2008. These figures help present why the business case for building relationships at work is so compelling.

The table below indicates three categories of possible responses to conflict. Taking time away from the workplace through fake illness falls within the 'passive' category and demonstrates a link and contribution to increased organisation costs.

Conflict responses

Passive	Aggressive	Unintentional
<ul><li>Avoiding personal contact</li><li>Writing emails instead of talking</li><li>Withholding information</li><li>Not returning messages</li><li>Delaying giving required support</li><li>Taking sick leave</li></ul>	<ul><li>Getting others to take sides</li><li>Shouting</li><li>Pre-empting</li><li>Threatening</li><li>Undermining your opponent's reputation</li></ul>	<ul><li>Sweaty palms</li><li>Nervous gestures</li><li>Closed body posture</li><li>Tense facial expressions</li></ul>

Current conflict resolution methods, which are based on principles of active listening, empathy, effective communication, collaborative group process, dialogue, facilitation, bias and prejudice reduction, creative problem solving, and mediation, can provide rich opportunities for individuals and organisations to effectively reduce their levels and costs of conflict.

Taking a preventative approach to conflict management will include creating responsive conflict management procedures, training employees and line managers to be peer mediators, and revitalising relationships and morale through the positive redirection and resolution of internal and external conflicts.

Why do we get stuck in conflict?

There are many reasons why we become stuck in impasse and are unable to put a stop to our own conflicts. Listed below are ten cited by Ken Cloke which are extremely useful.

1. *Conflict defines us and gives our life meaning*

Having an enemy is a quick, easy source of identity, because we are whatever they are not. By defining our opponents as evil, we implicitly define ourselves as good. Our opponents' apparently demonic behaviours allow us to appear – if not angelic by comparison – at least poor, innocent victims who are entitled to sympathy and support. Yet identifying ourselves as victims leaves us feeling powerless to resolve our disputes and encourages us to spiral downward into an abyss of fear, pain, anger and self righteousness from which it becomes more and more difficult to escape. It makes our opponents seem worse and ourselves better than we actually are. It causes us to lose perspective, resist learning, and hold onto unrealistic expectations.

2. *Conflict gives us energy*

Even if it is only the energy of anger, fear, jealousy, guilt, shame and grief. We can become addicted to the adrenalin rush, the flash point intensity and the intimacy of combat. Yet, this energy is ultimately debilitating, providing a quick stimulus that dies just as quickly, in place of the healthier, longer-lasting energy that emanates from compassion, collaboration, and honest empathetic communication. The negative energy in conflict can keep us stuck and deepen our suffering, causing us to pay a steep physical, intellectual, emotional and spiritual price in deteriorated health, reduced peace of mind, anxiety and unhappiness.

3. *Conflict ennobles our misery*

Conflict makes it appear that we are suffering for a worthwhile cause. Without conflict, we may feel we have suffered in vain and be forced to critique our choices and regret the wasted lives we've led. Yet the effort to assign higher meaning to our suffering encourages us to justify its continuation or to deceive ourselves into thinking our own abusive behaviours serve some higher purpose. It causes us to get angry at people who suggest alternatives and encourages us to hold onto our suffering, rather than learn from it, let it go and move on to more collaborative, less hostile relationships.

4.   *Conflict safeguards our personal space*

It also encourages others to recognise our needs and respect our privacy. For many of us, conflict seems the only way of effectively declaring our rights, securing the respect of others, restoring our inner balance, and protecting ourselves from boundary violations. Yet, conflict also creates false boundaries, keeps out those we want to let in and lets in those we don't, substitutes declarations of rights for satisfaction of interests, secures respect based on fear rather than personal regard, and creates justifications for counterattack and continued abuse. It erects walls that separate and isolate us from each other and prevent us from collaboratively negotiating the use of common space, being authentic, or finding out who we or who they actually are.

5.   *Conflict creates intimacy*

Even if it is only the transient, negative intimacy of fear, rage, attachment, and loss. Every two year old instinctively knows that it is better to be noticed for doing something wrong than not to be noticed at all. Yet negative intimacy is ultimately unsatisfactory because it prevents us from finding positive intimacy in its stead. Many relationships are sustained by invalidating, insulting, conflict-laden communications that simultaneously bring us together and keep us apart, frustrate our efforts to get closer and undermine the lasting intimacy we really want based on positive regard, mutual affection, trust and shared vulnerability.

6.   *Conflict camouflages our weaknesses*

Conflict does this by diverting attention away from sensitive subjects we would rather avoid discussing. It is a smokescreen, a way of passing the buck, blaming others and distracting attention from our mistakes. Yet doing so cheats us of opportunities to learn from our mistakes, makes us defensive, diminishes our integrity, and reduces our capacity for authentic, responsible relationships. It impedes our willingness to address real issues, and diverts our awareness from sensitive subjects, falsely magnifying their importance and effect.

7.   *Conflict powerfully communicates what we honestly feel*

This allows us to vent and assuage our pain by unloading our emotions onto others. While venting allows us to reduce our own emotional suffering, it increases stress and emotional suffering in others and fails to communicate our respect and regard for them. Venting encourages us not to take responsibility for our choices or address what got us upset in the first place. Venting communicates disrespect, encourages defensiveness and counterattack, escalates underlying conflicts, and does not accurately express who we are capable of being when we are with someone who is genuinely listening and caring.

8.   *Conflict gets results*

It forces others to heed us, especially faceless bureaucrats, clerks, and service representatives, who only seem to respond to our requests or do what we want when we yell at them. But, yelling turns us into angry, insensitive, aggravated people and adds unnecessary stress to the lives of frequently unhappy, alienated, powerless, poorly paid employees who are compelled to pointlessly accept our wrath. It turns us into bullies, and gets us less in the long run than we could get by politely requesting their assistance and eliciting their desire to be helpful. It discourages us from being genuine and open, and produces outcomes that undermine what we really want.

9.   *Conflict makes us feel righteous*

Conflict does this by encouraging us to believe that we are opposing evil behaviours and rewarding those that are good. Our opponents' pernicious actions justify us in giving them what they 'rightly deserve'. Yet righteousness is easily transformed into self-righteousness, and good and evil are far more complex, subtle and nuanced than we are prepared to admit. Engaging in conflict reduces our capacity for empathy and compassion. It makes us haughty, judgmental, superior and less able to be humble, accepting, and egalitarian in our relationships. And, it allows us to cross the line from punishing evil to committing it ourselves.

10.   *Conflict prompts change*

This feels better than impasse and stagnation. Many changes only take place as a result of conflict – not because it is actually necessary to achieve a given result, but because people's fear and resistance make it so. Yet conflict also prompts resistance to change, which can be more successfully overcome through inclusion, collaborative dialogue, and interest-based negotiations. Adversarial conflict stimulates a backlash dedicated to minimising whatever gains it may achieve and polarising those who might otherwise become its supporters. Worse, as a means, it undermines the ends to which it is ostensibly dedicated. While the deepest and most consequential changes actually require conflict, understanding this requirement allows us to design strategies for transforming destructive criticisms into constructive suggestions for improvement and increasing our skills and effectiveness as agents of change.

The list of ten statements serves as a comprehensive, almost cathartic record of views on the realities of conflict and its potential impact. When we encounter conflict we can choose to face it and deal with it, or we see it as a nuisance and hope it disappears. Likewise, we can also view conflict as a learning opportunity to discover more about ourselves.

The Concept of Mediation

An Overview

Mediation is a voluntary process for resolving disputes in which another person helps the parties negotiate a settlement. Mediation is **voluntary** in the sense that in the majority of cases it takes place as a result of the parties agreeing to enter the mediation process. It cannot happen if one or more of the parties refuse to participate, although it is quite possible that parties who initially refuse may agree to mediation at a later stage.

Recently, non-voluntary mediations have taken place. These happen when parties are required by a court or contract to mediate before or instead of arbitration or litigation.

Mediation is **non-binding** unless and until an agreement is reached. The agreement then becomes an enforceable contract. Until this point, parties may walk away from the mediation at any time as entering the process itself does not bind any party to settlement. It is important to note, however, that signing up to mediation does not mean that an employee gives up their statutory rights. This means that in the event that a settlement agreement for a workplace mediation dispute breaks down, the parties (and organisation) have two options. Firstly, to attempt mediation again, or secondly, to invoke the organisation's disciplinary or performance management procedures.

Whilst parties are expected to sign a settlement agreement in workplace mediation cases, the contract is more of a psychological one.

Under the Globis Mediation Group mediation procedure, agreements have to be in writing and signed to be legally binding.

The mediator is a **neutral person** who is there to assist the parties in their negotiations. The mediator provides a clear head, impartiality, process management, encouragement, optimism, and above all, brings hope to situations that may seem hopeless, whilst always leaving the problem and the decision to settle in the hands of the parties. A skilled mediator doesn't necessarily need to be an expert or specialist in the field to which the dispute is linked.

Mediation is **private,** conducted without prejudice and with total confidentiality. The results are rarely made public, although they can be publicised if both parties agree.

The Mediation Process

Mediators often speak reverently about 'trusting the process'. There are many examples of mediations where parties begin the mediation bitter and entrenched, but by mid-morning the same parties become engaged in productive, sometimes friendly discussions. A broad framework for the mediation process has been defined over time. Mediation is a flexible process and, with experience, a mediator can use that flexibility to their advantage.

Prior to any workplace mediation taking place, the mediator should make preliminary contact with the parties. The principal reasons for the contact are:

- To confirm agreement to the mediation
- To understand the nature of the conflict
- To agree terms for the mediation including dates, times, location, duration, and documentation
- To outline how the mediation process works

If the mediator is external to the organisation, issues such as mediation costs should be discussed with the stakeholder who is authorising the process to take place.

The core of the mediation session is then made up of a number of elements. These include:

- Opening statements – outlining the process and the role of the mediator.

- Uninterrupted time – giving each party an opportunity to express the key points about the conflict.

- The exchange – held either as joint meetings or private confidential meetings (called caucuses) between the mediator and each party separately.

- Exploring the options – attempting to shift the discussion into the future e.g. what would you like to see happen? What would prevent this situation from happening again?

- Constructing the agreement – beginning to document ideas for solutions and testing thoughts with each party.

- Writing the agreement – when parties agree to settle, it is the responsibility of the mediator to draft an agreement that is a true reflection of settlement points.

- Closing the mediation – thanking the parties for their engagement in the process.

The Mediator's Role
The mediator fulfils several important roles. The mediator is:

- A manager of the process; providing firm but sensitive control, conveying confidence that the process is yielding fruit and maintaining momentum and a sense of progress.

- A facilitator; helping the parties to overcome deadlock and to find a way of working co-operatively towards a settlement that is mutually acceptable.

- An information gatherer; absorbing and organising data and identifying common ground.

- A reality tester; helping the parties to take a private realistic view, rather than public open scrutiny.

- A problem solver; bringing a clear and creative mind to help the parties construct an outcome that best meets their needs.

- A sponge that soaks up all the frustrations, emotions and uncertainties of the parties and helps them channel their energy in more positive ways.

- A scribe who writes or helps write the terms of any settlement agreement ensuring it is clear.

- A settlement prompter; who if no agreement is reached at the mediation, will help parties to keep the momentum towards settlement.

It is important that the mediator gains the trust of the parties and that he/she is competent enough to fulfil the required role. When parties trust the mediator they are much more likely to disclose information relevant to the settlement of the dispute.

Why Mediation Works

There are a number of advantages to mediating a dispute rather than litigating. These include:

- *Speed of dispute resolution*
  People do not like being in conflict. It is worrying, time consuming and a drain on both financial and management resources. Mediation sessions can be set up very quickly - within days if necessary.

- *Mediation does not affect statutory or human rights*
  The mediation process can run in tandem with the grievance and disciplinary process. As it is without prejudice, mediation poses little or no risk to parties who engage in the process.

- *Cost Savings*
  Issues can be settled quickly and can avoid direct and/or indirect costs.

- *It improves communications*
  People in conflict tend to take up rigid positions and will avoid communicating with the party with whom they are in conflict or communicate to them through an intermediary. The face-to-face meeting which occurs at the joint session allows open communication directly between the parties again. This can help ensure that methods for prevention of conflicts arising in the future are addressed within the process.

- *It unearths the real issues*
  The mediator helps parties to focus on the real issues in their dispute. Having got the parties to agree to mediation, the mediator starts to move the parties to settlement. Sometimes, if mediation does not settle on the day, it is because only now the real issues have been discovered, one or both parties may wish to discuss these with colleagues before continuing. A second session may of course be set up by the mediator.

Mediation Style

Globis Mediation Group subscribes to facilitative (as opposed to evaluative) mediation as the preferred style. Facilitative mediation means that the mediator offers a structured process for the parties to make their own decisions. Evaluative mediators tend to be legal practitioners who may offer direction to a settlement and advise on the likely outcome of a court scenario. There are situations, however, when the boundaries may become blurred. For example, certain types of questions or the level to which reality testing is undertaken may be considered to be evaluative.

Mediators must be careful not to be perceived as judgmental in any way. Facilitative mediation supports this objective. It requires the mediator to be discreet in presence, allowing the parties to achieve settlement simply by greasing the wheels of communication. It is important, however, to note that simply by being 'present', it is unlikely that any dispute will move towards settlement. Mediation is hard work and hardest of all on the mediator. It is the mediator who must front all the stages of the process, such as chairing the meetings, setting the direction, thinking through strategies, soaking up the emotion, the facts and arguments. It is also the mediator who has to check any issues of confidentiality and remain as alert at the end of the day, as at the start. Based on this pressure, the mediator may become tempted to offer the parties thoughts or suggestions for settlement. This must not happen in any circumstances. The dispute should always remain the responsibility of the parties to settle. It is upon this principle that mediation rests differently to other forms of ADR.

This can cause some people, such as those in the legal profession and HR advisors, difficulty as mediators. This is because their day job requires them to give their views and opinions and they may continue to see it as their duty to do so. If in mediation, however, parties want expert or legal advice, they should seek it from an advisor, not the mediator.

It is the responsibility of the mediator to ensure that parties attend the mediation with a full understanding of the mediator's role and the responsibility placed upon them (the parties) to attempt to find solutions to their dispute.

Whilst the mediator should not give advice on any course of action a party might take, they do have a role to play in 'reality-testing', questioning and challenging to help parties to be flexible in attempting to solve their dispute.

Facilitative mediation is an active and strenuous process requiring much alertness and concentration from the mediator, sometimes over many hours. A mediator must engage their skills as advanced communicator and problem solver, as well as the willingness to avoid dictating, in preference for supporting the process.

The Phases of the Mediation

The LAETR™ Mediation Cycle has been developed based on Globis Mediation Group's extensive experience within mediation. Using the **LAETR™ Mediation Cycle** during workplace mediation training courses helps delegates understand the process for helping to resolve differences in the workplace. This model has been used in many workplace mediations with notable success.

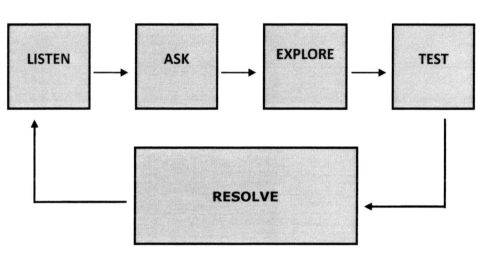

The LAETR™ Model

Listen:	Listening within another person's frame of reference to fully understand the issues that have led to the dispute
Ask:	Ask appropriate and relevant questions that help clarify understanding of the background to the dispute
Explore:	Explore options for resolution that will help the parties focus on the future rather than on the past
Test:	Test and reality-check that any potential solutions have been thought through and are workable for the parties
Resolve:	Resolve the dispute by summarising the parties' positions and bringing the mediation to an appropriate close

This is a good time at which to outline the things that mediation is not:

Mediation is not a soft option
Organisations are entitled to invoke and enforce organisational processes such as the grievance and disciplinary procedure, instead of conflict resolution principles such as mediation. Where an employee may be in dispute with the employer, the employer may feel that it has acted properly in every sense and that an employment tribunal should decide who may have been right or wrong. This may be an appropriate course of action where the organisation wants to send a message to its employees about its willingness to defend itself. Even if an organisation wins its legal process, it must of course weigh up the costs of such action and consider whether this is the best use of its resources.

Mediation is not a bar to litigation
Mediation does not preclude the use of other methods of dispute resolution. In some cases an action may have commenced before mediation is adopted. Proceedings may or may not be stayed pending the outcome of the mediation. Parties may also want to begin litigation to demonstrate seriousness and engage with mediation to obtain a more secure, viable and speedy result.

Mediation is not a waste of time and money if it fails
If settlement is not reached in mediation, it is often reached soon afterwards. This is mainly because it has been a tool to surface the issues on which the dispute has been based. Parties then have better clarification on these issues and then after reflection may choose to move to settle issues of difference.

Mediation is not a sign of weakness or for 'wimps'
The value of using mediation as a conflict resolution tool can be financially proven. In an environment where a return on investment is critical for business leaders, mediation is a justifiable investment. Mediation helps to reduce unproductive management time and enhances the skills of line managers and the HR function. It is a period of concentrated negotiation that requires agility of thought, flexibility and imagination. It is hard work, intellectually, physically and emotionally, for everyone involved.

Mediation is not counselling
The mediator and counsellor share a number of core skills. Their roles, however, are completely different. Both mediation and counselling can take various forms but, in general, the mediator preserves a neutral relationship with the parties, whereas the counsellor develops what can sometimes be described as an intense

relationship with the client. The mediator uses problem-solving techniques; the counsellor applies psychological analysis; the mediator acknowledges feelings, whereas the counsellor explores emotions.

The mediator operates by a principle called 'omni-partiality', which means being on both sides at the same time. This is not an easy skill to develop but develops over time through experience.

Mediation in the Workplace

Resistance to addressing conflict in organisations is similar to the resistance that divides nations and communities. As organisations become more complex, they fragment and become more insular, creating silos with their own pockets of tribal language that can exclude particular individuals or groups.

The uptake of mediation and conflict resolution practices in the UK has been slow, although the public sector has picked it up much more quickly than the private sector. One of the possible reasons for this is the willingness of some sections of the private sector to throw money at problems to go away, through things such as compromise agreements.

Whilst this provides a temporary reprieve, it is unlikely to unearth and provide a solution for what might be ingrained cultural issues within an organisation. Therefore, the organisation enters a cycle of throwing money at problems which are likely to continually linger below the surface. This is also a method of rewarding poor management and systems. In the most extreme cases, this could lead to problems such as those faced by Enron in 2002. Documents show that at Enron, simply talking about what was going on was off limits. Organisations that fail to support open communications are doomed to fail. With the emergence of more and more data on the costs of conflict, organisations are likely to embrace the worth of mediation more over the next few years.

Positioning the business case for an organisation to adopt the principles of mediation is much more likely to succeed when cost savings can be demonstrated and successful cases shown.

There are a number of ways to bring the fundamentals of mediation into organisations. Perhaps the most effective way is to incorporate mediation clauses into contracts of employment and staff handbooks. This then becomes the reference point for any dispute or point of difference.

Workplace or Employment Mediation?
Often two terms are used interchangeably for mediating disputes at work. The two terms, however, have different meanings:

- Workplace mediation refers to a dispute that relates to an individual who is still employed with their organisation.
- Employment mediation refers to a dispute where an employee has left an organisation.

The difference is important to note as there are some issues a mediator will experience when conducting an employment mediation that they may not experience when undertaking a workplace or internal mediation. Three examples of this are interaction with lawyers, issues about legal costs and arrangements for a party exiting an organisation as part of a settlement. In employment mediation cases, the mediation commissioner is much more likely to be an employment lawyer.

The mediation is often more commercially focused and leans more towards negotiation. The mediator will have to work with both the parties and their legal representatives, and will have to understand potential compensation. When reality-checking, the mediator may also refer to case law. Arrangements for compromise agreements to be drafted will also have to be made.

In workplace mediation there is much more of a requirement to work with people's emotions and consider potential cultural issues. Mediators will often have to exercise large amounts of patience when dealing with parties and their emotions. The mediator will also have to think about potential flaws in the organisational structure that may have led or contributed to the dispute in the first place. In this sense, the mediator can also become an advisor to the organisation.

Internal or External Mediator?

There are a number of considerations for the organisation when deciding to appoint an internal (an employee of the organisation) or external mediator, such as:

Internal or external mediator?
Internal
Knows and understands the organisational culture
Potentially requires less briefing
Little or no cost
May not be perceived as impartial
May have historical baggage
Experience level may be low
External
Comes with little or no knowledge of the organisation or parties in dispute
May be a more experienced mediator with the ability to pick up issues quickly
Charges for services
Likely to gain trust of parties
Able to provide the organisation with a fresh view of possible cultural or organisational issues

Leaving the competency of the mediator aside, it is ultimately the choice of the organisation to decide which option will work best, based on the merits of each case. An organisation with a high number of employees who have been trained in the skills of mediation and conflict resolution is likely to experience far fewer ongoing issues than those without.

Once an agreement has been reached to engage in mediation, there are a number of steps the workplace mediator should follow. These include:

- Understanding the brief from the mediation commissioner
- Having preliminary discussions with the parties
- Choosing the location
- The phases of the mediation
- Advising the organisation on issues for future prevention

Understanding the brief from the mediation commissioner

The mediation commissioner is the person requesting the mediation intervention. This could be the line manager and/or someone from the HR function. It is important that the mediator understands the issues surrounding the need for mediation from this person. It is advisable to have a face to face meeting for this, but it is not always necessary, especially for more experienced mediators.

This discussion should provide answers to questions such as:

- What is the background to the dispute?
- What is the current situation?
- Have the parties agreed to mediation?

As mediator, it is important to get an understanding of the facts from the commissioner's perspective. Issues of hearsay, gossip and rumour may come up, but the mediator should refrain from engaging in such details. The mediator would also use this session to discuss the contract for the mediation.

If the dispute relates to a former employee, issues such as legal fees should form part of the discussion.

Preliminary discussions with the parties

It is important that the mediator has preliminary discussions with each party separately. The purpose of these discussions is to:

- Allow the mediator to introduce themselves to each party
- Find out each party's view on the background to the conflict
- Explain how the mediation process works
- Establish whether each party is ready for a joint meeting
- Determine the best way to approach next steps
- Discuss arrival times (schedule a 20 minute gap between each party)

Choosing the location
Globis Mediation Group advises that workplace mediations are conducted away from the parties' normal place of work. The best facility is a neutral location with a comfortable room and appropriate furniture. Each party should have a similar room that can be used as their private base and which the mediator can use for caucus meetings. Each room should also have an adequate supply of refreshments.

The phases of the mediation
Usually the mediation will follow a three stage process:

- Opening phase
- Private sessions (caucuses)
- Joint session

Opening phase
Before the parties arrive:

- Arrange the rooms: chairs, tables, lighting, room temperature, privacy, flip charts etc. There should be a room for each party and one for the mediator

- Carry out a final review of any notes, memorise names and job titles

- Check the venue for all facilities and conveniences

When the parties arrive, meet each party at the reception point of the venue. Use the 20 minute gap to settle the first arriving party and go over the stages of the mediation process. This is also a good time to get the mediation agreement signed and check for any questions the party may have since the last contact.

Give both parties the time to be settled before calling them to the first joint session. One of the ways in which the mediator can encourage and enhance the informal approach is by setting up the room for the opening joint session.

Guidance notes:

- Be willing to maintain firm management over the proceedings – the parties will look to you to exercise control and will respect you for doing it

- Use your intuition – even though there is a scripted process for mediations, situations may sometimes arise which require creative thinking

- Keep note taking to a minimum – note the essential points and make more detailed notes during breaks between meetings

Mediator's opening

The mediator's opening has four main purposes:

- To set the tone of the mediation
- To establish the mediator's authority as manager of the process
- To inform the parties about the mediation process
- To establish ground rules for the mediation

Welcome

The mediator's opening is important as it should be used to help establish an environment that will be conducive for discussion and resolution. A poor opening could sufficiently harm the credibility of the mediator enough to impede the process.

Welcome the parties individually. Keep in mind that the parties are likely to be tense, wary and sceptical. Whilst the mediator is well versed in the mediation process, this is likely to be the first time that the parties have participated in such a process.

Purpose of the mediation

The mediator should use the opening to clarify neutrality and explain the mediator's role. The mediator's role is to facilitate a process that will surface issues of the conflict and ideally lead to a resolution of those issues. The mediator's role is not to impose a solution. It is the parties' problem and it will be their solution.

Forms and logistics

The parties should have the time they need to review any mediation documentation. Parties should be made aware of the location of all facilities and conveniences. The mediator should give an indication of timeframe for the process. This should include separate (caucus) meetings. This is where the mediator quite literally uses shuttle diplomacy, going between the parties' rooms until it is appropriate for the parties to engage in a joint meeting. Mediation is a voluntary process and parties may leave at any time if they are unhappy with the mediation.

Confidentiality

Maintaining confidentiality is a crucial factor for the mediation process to work. As mediator, it is wise to be explicit in the opening about what can and cannot be repeated during the mediation. Confidentiality works on two levels:

- The entire mediation is confidential to those taking part, unless there is an explicit agreement to publicise any resolution.

- Information given to the mediator in private caucus is confidential between the mediator and the party. This is crucial. If this aspect is broken, it will be impossible to regain it and the mediation may have to be deferred and a different mediator appointed.

Another tip on confidentiality is that you, as mediator, should also keep any notes concealed. Remember that some people can read upside down text very well.

In workplace mediation, an additional factor to consider is how any feedback will be given to the organisation. Most organisations would expect some level of information about the outcome of the mediation. One way to deal with this is to agree with the parties what can and cannot be shared. Where settlement is reached, parties are normally willing for the settlement agreement to be shared with the organisation.

Parties' opening comments

The parties' opening comments give everyone at the table – the parties and the mediator – the chance to hear each party's case. The mediator will get an overview of the mood, whilst also learning a little about the personalities present. Equally as important, each party, perhaps for the first time, has the opportunity to hear the other party's view of the conflict. It has been known for mediations to resolve issues at this stage of the process, as parties are often unaware of the details or severity of conflict. Once the specifics are heard, it can cause some parties to offer an apology and hand of reconciliation.

It is important that during the mediator's opening comments, the mediator restates to the parties that they will have the opportunity to outline their case, uninterrupted. This opening session of the mediation enables:

- The mediator to set the ground rules
- The parties to state their side of the story

As part of the mediator's opening, he/she should state:

'Please respect each person's turn to speak, even though it may be difficult to listen without responding straight away. You should feel free to take notes for yourself about anything you want to discuss later'.

The speakers

The person who is most aggrieved or has been instrumental in requesting the mediation should speak first. In commercial mediations, this would be 'the claimant'. The mediator should inform the parties who will be required to speak first, so it isn't a surprise when both parties are together.

There may be occasions when it becomes difficult for the listening party to contain themselves from commenting. If this happens, firmly remind the interrupting party that they will have their turn to speak as soon as the other party has finished.

Once both parties have spoken, it is the judgment of the mediator to decide whether dialogue should continue as a joint session. This can be helpful to continue exposing any issues that came up during the opening comments. It can be fatal if ill-judged. Experienced mediators will develop an instinct for the appropriateness of such a continuation.

Private sessions (Caucuses)

Caucus sessions usually follow the joint opening session and allow the mediator to explore issues further and discuss thoughts following the joint session. The mediator should remember during these sessions to check information that should remain confidential. The caucus sessions are also the forum for reality-checking. Reality-checking allows the mediator to help parties think through potential ramifications of failing to resolve a dispute or going to litigation. Reality-checking can be extremely helpful in moving towards resolution, but the mediator walks a tight rope when doing so. Push too hard and the party may feel that you are not taking them seriously, or that you are taking sides with the other party. Any suspicion of this can damage the credibility of the mediator. If the mediator, however, fails to reality-check appropriately, they do a disservice to the party and the mediation may never reach its objective of resolving, rather than settling the conflict.

Joint session

The joint session which follows the caucus sessions should be used to continue exploring issues or move to resolution. The mediator would have been sharing information from the caucus sessions through 'shuttle diplomacy' between the parties. Sometimes the information that has been raised during the caucus sessions may cause a party to push for a joint session to discuss 'new' understandings.

There is no rule on whether the mediator should use caucus or joint sessions; it is a matter of what is appropriate at the time. The main disadvantage of a joint session is that parties will not give sensitive or confidential information to the mediator in the presence of the other party.

Where it appears that there is likely to be an ongoing working relationship, it is advisable to get the parties together at the earliest moment. Many workplace mediations are conducted as joint sessions. The mediator may realise during the opening that the parties are at the stage where they are willing to talk to each other. In these types of cases, the mediator's role might oscillate between mediation and facilitation.

Moving towards resolution
The resolution of a workplace dispute may vary depending on whether there is the intention for an ongoing relationship. For example, an appropriate conclusion to a dispute may be that one or both parties (if the conflict is between two people) leave the organisation. In this case, the mediator may move to discussions with the said party about terms on which any termination may take place.

The ideal situation in any mediation is to secure a 'win-win' solution. Any win-win agreement is likely to involve the requirement for either or both parties to 'give something up'. It is useful for the mediator to summarise issues as the discussion progresses. Where there are numerous issues, it is often helpful to 'cluster' them to make it easier to work through. Where it becomes clear that the interests for each party are becoming aligned, the mediator should begin to document them for the party/ies to see. This will help put issues where there appears to be agreement to one side, and then the mediator can begin working on other areas.

Depending on the number of issues being discussed, the mediator follows this process until there is clarity that all issues have been highlighted, discussed and resolved.

The Negotiation (Exploration) Phase in Mediation

In the negotiation (or exploration) phase of the mediation there are two strands that are important to the mediator. These are:

- Understanding the parties' negotiating strategies; and

- Using your own negotiating skills to present, reframe or help craft settlement possibilities

Caucus meetings, joint sessions and working groups can all be valuable during negotiation.

Caucus meetings
Sometimes you may need to work actively to help parties recognise that settlement is in their best interests. Parties can have difficulty moving from entrenched positions to a more flexible and open view about options for resolution. Your understanding of negotiation and negotiating strategies will be very important during this stage. During private meetings in the negotiation phase the mediator may help in:

- Identifying items of differing value; one party may place little value on something considered important by the other party

- Prioritising parties' concerns and aspirations

- Being a sounding board and allowing parties to vent their feelings and test out their positions

- Reality-testing – holding a mirror up to the party and asking how realistic a particular statement or position might be

- Exploring the cost of continued litigation or arbitration

- Shaping proposals that meet the other party's needs

The mediator has a key role as reality-tester. It is not uncommon for a party who has been advocating a position for some time to become blind to facts that may be inconsistent with that position. As a neutral person you may be able to point out in an objective way, facts that a party may be overlooking. One of the functions of a mediator is to help the parties change what might be a one-dimensional perspective and begin to understand what common interests they share. As the mediation progresses, parties will permit or even request that the mediator passes on information or offers. It is important that you maintain your role as a facilitator of the process. You may, for example, choose to store the information that has been given to you for later use, or even feel that using the information may not add value to the mediation process. As mediator, you are in the unique position of piecing together the jigsaw and will be in a good position to judge whether information will help or hinder.

Joint sessions
Following the initial joint session, many mediators – particularly those with little experience - may choose to conduct the whole mediation in caucus sessions, shuttling between the parties throughout the day. Joint sessions, however, can play a role if you feel that the parties are ready for it. If you intend to hold a joint session it is important to remember that the parties are unlikely to give confidential information to the mediator in the presence of the other party. The advantages of a joint session are that:

- It allows parties to talk directly to each other to outline their position
- It allows parties to negotiate directly
- It can boost the momentum of the mediation
- It can break deadlock by allowing parties to give explanations on specific issues

Getting into deadlock
The main reason parties come to mediation is because they have reached deadlock in their own negotiations. There is the potential for deadlock in any negotiation. In some cases it is inevitable; in others it could be deliberate. Parties can get into deadlock for some of the following reasons:

- Parties become *entrenched* in their positions, digging in and conceding nothing.

- It may be that one party has reached their *bottom line* and has nowhere else to go. The climate of negotiation in our culture expects 'give and take'. When one party stops at an early stage, even if a reasonable solution has been tabled, the other side may interpret this as not playing fair and see the first party as being unreasonable.

- *Emotional baggage* - all negotiations carry some element of emotion. Parties have their own pressures: a reputation to maintain, career to preserve, ambition or matters of principle they want adhered to.

- *Team dynamics* - deadlock can be common in team negotiations because the risk is compounded. There can often be the temptation to 'perform' in front of colleagues to impress and gain approval.

- *Tactical deadlock* - enforcing a delay prolongs the waiting and can put pressure on the other party to soften and concede more.

- *There is the need to save face* - we often spend much of our life creating safeguards against losing face, to preserve our credibility and dignity. Most of our responses in this area are automatic and pre-conditioned. As a mediator, it is important to be sensitive to this and ensure that the need for saving face is met during the mediation process. This is likely to help you to help the parties move towards settlement.

Breaking deadlock

Settlement rarely comes easily and having patience and stamina as a mediator will greatly improve your success rate. Deadlock may have arisen because of animosity or other ill-feeling between individuals on opposite sides. A mediator can help break situations of deadlock by:

- Helping the parties to shift from positional to principled negotiation, from competitive to co-operative mode and to seeing this as a joint problem that can be solved jointly.

- Allowing the venting of emotion. If strong feelings are suppressed or unacknowledged they may be a block to progress; preventing full participation in the process.

- Finding a concession that is low cost but high value. Not all issues in negotiations are of equal value to each party.

- Taking a break; allowing emotions to cool and giving time to reassess positions will help the process. It could also be helpful to put particular issues of difficulty to one side and revisit them later on to allow progress to be made in other areas.

- Introducing wit and humour. If appropriate, consider telling a funny story and saying something light hearted. This will momentarily allow the parties' minds to come away from the dispute and give respite for relaxation.

- Breaking down the problem. Clustering and compartmentalising the issues often helps parties deal with problems, as it allows them to focus on one set of things at a time.

- Changing strategy. If you are taking an approach that isn't working, then do something else.

- Introduce a deadline. This is helpful as it focuses the minds of the parties to work to an imposed timescale. This can of course be moved if need be.

- Highlight progress made so far. This will help the move towards problem-solving.

- Introduce new information or reframe the issues that have been causing the blockage so that they carry different weight or perspective.

- Intervention by more senior executives. Sometimes a more senior person might be needed to impose or approve next steps.

Breaking deadlock can often be a problem because neither side wants to 'go first'. There will always be difficulties, but the mediator carries the responsibility of thinking about creative solutions that will help free up a process that has stalled.

Getting to settlement
Mediation is a great tool for pursuing win-win solutions and producing an outcome that leaves both parties satisfied. However, the mediation process often brings pain as both parties may need to 'give something up' in order to reach an agreed settlement.

In general, to help move towards settlement, the mediator should:

- Avoid bottom lines - despite attempting to build a relationship with the parties to get them to trust you, any bottom line figure that you are told is likely to move as the day progresses. So, be careful about how you choose to use 'bottom line' figures.

- Leave the figures until later in the day - it can be tempting for parties to go straight to the figures and begin a negotiated settlement as quickly as possible. This usually fails. Parties want the opportunity to express themselves and talk about what has led them to get to the point at which mediation is necessary. Moving to discuss figures too quickly is likely to mean that you lose precious ground and may have to go back to a previous stage of the process.

- Think about conveying offer s - as mediator, you are in total control of the process. As you get to the stage where offers are being put on the table, you might feel delighted that this stage has started and begin to relay these offers between the parties. How and when figures are conveyed may make the difference to whether mediation settles or not. The mediator can use various strategies at this stage including:

  - Persuading each party to give a figure that cannot be disclosed to the other party until authorised

  - Reserving judgment on when to disclose a settlement figure, even if authorised to do so

  - Judging carefully whether any figure would be seen as derisory by the other party

  - Working out a strategy to close the gap between the parties as the mediation progresses

  - Being careful not to be 'used' by one of the parties, simply to find out the other party's bottom line figure

- Not impose settlements - it is of utmost importance that any settlement is the parties' own and not suggested or recommended by the mediator. If the mediator suggests a settlement, the parties may accept this and then recoil at a later stage because they don't own it. It might take time for the parties to get to a position that, as mediator, you feel they should arrive at, but it is much more likely to stick if the parties suggest it.

- Respect confidentiality - confidentiality is one of the sacred rules of mediation that should never be broken. It is always best to check what information the parties want treated as confidential. It is possible that mediation will break down if the mediator divulges information that was deemed confidential to any of the parties. The mediator could quite easily make a mistake or believe that it is worth taking the risk. Either way, if the confidence is broken and discovered by the party, the mediator will struggle to win back the trust and respect of the wronged party.

- Obtain settlement authority - in some cases, both financial and non-financial settlements may need to be approved. In some cases, the person attending the mediation can do this. In others, they may have to refer back to the organisation. It is important to check issues of authority at the start of the process. This should be done sensitively and in private, so as not to openly challenge the parties' authority and credibility.

- Remain optimistic - most mediations will hit a low point. At this stage you will be wondering whether you, as mediator, will be able to get a settlement to the dispute, and perhaps even question your own competence. The important thing to do is remain optimistic and keep your mind on settlement. Perseverance and determination will help you to keep moving towards settlement.

The Mediation Settlement Agreement

It is important that any mediation is documented and summarised by a mediation agreement. It is the responsibility of the mediator to ensure that this happens. Mediation is voluntary and without prejudice, so the content of any mediation cannot be discussed at any future tribunal or court hearing. Failure of the mediator to conduct a mediation underpinned by the appropriate documentation could bring unwelcome consequences.

Here is an example from a well documented commercial mediation. In the case of *Farm Assist (FAL) v Defra*, a mediation was held in June 2003, which led to a settlement. About four years later, FAL, having since gone into liquidation, asserted through its liquidator that the mediated settlement agreement had been procured by DEFRA through "economic duress" and should therefore be set aside. DEFRA, concerned both by the allegation and by the delay in making it, sought disclosure of all documents in FAL's possession which impinged upon the advice given by lawyers and experts which had led to their decision to settle with DEFRA at the mediation.

This included the legal advice given to FAL and its officers on the interpretation of a key contract; the advice given on the merits of claims, on offers to be made to DEFRA and responses to be made to counter-offers made by DEFRA; and advice given during and after the mediation, whether or not the mediator was present. FAL objected to disclosure of the advice tendered by their lawyers and insolvency advisors, on the grounds that legal professional privilege protected it from disclosure. DEFRA argued that FAL had effectively waived their right to assert such privilege by bringing proceedings against them in a way which made material the state of mind of the directing minds of FAL before and at the mediation.

Mr Justice Ramsey held that such advice was not disclosable by FAL to DEFRA by virtue of legal professional privilege. But he refused to strike out the claim for economic duress, and hence the question arose of proving by other means what happened at the mediation. The mediator could well be a material witness as to the nature of any alleged pressure brought to bear by DEFRA on FAL by way of economic duress. They will have chaired joint meetings at which significant remarks will have been made, and carried both those and any further arguments and the proposed terms of settlement between the parties. There has been no reported case hitherto in the UK of a mediator actually having given evidence so far, despite some close-run occasions.

The written and signed mediation agreement of 2003 provided for confidentiality as to the fact that the mediation took place and as to all information arising in relation to it including settlement terms, specific "without prejudice" privilege, and for the mediator not to be called "as a witness, consultant, arbitrator or expert in any litigation or arbitration in relation to the Dispute, and the Mediator will not act voluntarily in any such capacity without the written agreement of all the parties".

In the end, the matter was settled without the mediator having to give evidence to Justice Ramsey about matters relating to the mediation. However, it was a huge signal to mediators about the importance of robust processes and the importance of a signed mediation agreement being in place.

Globis Mediation Group has refused to conduct workplace mediations where either party is unwilling to sign a mediation agreement.

An organisation can choose the wording of their own mediation agreement but it is advised that some key points are included in any agreement. Globis Mediation Group provides template documentation to all its clients and course delegates.

The key points of an agreement would be that:

- The mediation is without prejudice
- The mediation is non-binding up until the point of agreement
- The mediator is named
- The parties are entitled to seek independent legal advice prior to the mediation
- The mediation is confidential

A copy of a mediation agreement can be seen at the end of this handbook.

For some parties, documenting the conclusion of a mediation session can feel incredibly formal. If there is unwillingness, it may suggest that resolution has not quite been reached. The mediation agreement will provide a point of reference for the parties, the mediation commissioner and the mediator. It is good practice for mediators of workplace disputes to check how well the process has worked with the mediation commissioner and parties three months after the mediation.

A mediation settlement agreement which is written up at the end of a workplace mediation session may include aspects such as:

- Fred agrees to use face to face, two-way conversation rather than email for work updates

- Jane agrees to keep all conversations with Fred on a business and appropriate level

- Fred agrees to draft a departmental organisation chart by 23 February

- Jane agrees that the agenda for team meetings will be circulated at least 48 hours ahead of any meeting

A mediation settlement agreement which is written at the end of an employment mediation session may include aspects such as:

- The organisation agrees to pay Bill £25,000 in lieu of notice within 28 days of the date of this agreement

- It is deemed that the above payment can be made on a tax-free basis

- The organisation agrees to provide a reference as worded in annex "a"

- The parties agree that a company announcement will be made in line with annex "b"

- The organisation agrees to continue providing private medical care for the next two months after the date of the mediated settlement agreement

- The organisation agrees to pay Bill's legal costs in relation to the dispute up to the value of £5,500 to paid within 28 days of the date of this agreement

The point of any agreement is that it is symbolic of closure, resolution, captures the main points of the workplace dispute and provides a document which can be used by the parties in any ongoing review. It is imperative that the agreement reflects an accurate summary of the conclusion of the mediated discussion.

After the mediation
Where the mediation has proved successful, parties will have signed a settlement agreement and shaken hands.

In cases where settlement isn't reached, the mediator should work with the parties and mediation commissioner on appropriate next steps. These could include returning to work with each individual for longer periods of time before any joint meetings are renegotiated. There is always a danger in leaving any interaction with parties who have not been able to settle their dispute, that emotions become more entrenched. The sooner the mediator can re-engage the better.

The Mediator's Skill Set

Through its training process, Globis Mediation Group uses seven competencies to provide course delegates with the opportunity to develop the full range of skills necessary to become effective workplace mediators.

A competency can be defined as a set of behaviour patterns that a person needs in order to perform a certain task effectively. The fact that competencies define tasks in terms of behaviours is extremely useful, because behaviours can be learnt and developed. Thus, Globis Mediation Group mediator competencies give you a blueprint of the behaviours that you need to develop in order to become an effective mediator.

Mediator competencies

Planning and Organising
Plans and organises the mediation process so that it runs smoothly. The mediator who is excellent at planning and organising:

- Engages with the mediation commissioner; explaining the process
- Spends time seeking to understand the issues
- Holds pre-mediation discussions, with the parties, unearthing issues relating to the conflict
- Puts the parties at ease, providing a thorough understanding of the workplace mediation process
- On the day of the mediation, ensures that the physical surroundings are well prepared

Managing the Process
Demonstrates confidence in handling the process, keeping free on content. The mediator who is excellent at process management:

- Sets clear ground rules in the opening statement and ensures the parties stick to those rules (for example, ensuring that opening statements are made without interruption)
- Ensures that momentum is maintained by focussing on the issues
- Strictly maintains confidentiality in private sessions
- Keeps parties informed of what is happening
- Ensures that whilst parties are not in private session they are engaged in

tasks relevant to resolving the dispute
- Terminates a mediation if it is appropriate to do so

Communication

The mediator demonstrates excellent skills in listening, questioning and communicating both verbally and non-verbally. The mediator who is an excellent communicator:

- Demonstrates deep listening, gives positive visual and verbal cues and summarises to ensure full understanding
- Motivates parties to participate actively and co-operatively
- Uses different types of question appropriately – e.g. open, closed, probing
- Uses open and positive body language
- Reframes effectively
- Is sensitive to cultural differences when communicating
- Is sensitive to the body language of others
- Uses silence positively
- Empathises with the parties and makes positive efforts to develop rapport with them
- Listens to and thereby understands each party's situation and feelings
- Is able, when necessary, to effectively summarise, paraphrase and reframe statements, views and opinions expressed by parties

Creativity

The mediator is not restricted by procedures or tied into certain ways of looking at things. The mediator who is creative:

- Encourages parties into a problem-solving mode
- Consciously uses tools to encourage creativity in parties (e.g. brainstorming)
- Encourages parties to look at disputes from different angles
- Is prepared to put forward options to resolve disputes, but does not try to "sell" the parties a preferred solution
- Tests the workability of proposed settlements
- Has a variety of strategies available to resolve an impasse
- Is flexible when applying the mediation process

Facilitating

The mediator encourages and enables parties to reach an agreement that is mutually acceptable. The mediator who is an excellent facilitator:

- Consciously develops an atmosphere conducive to parties moving towards settlement
- Is seen by all parties to be neutral, and treats all parties the same
- Ensures that all parties have opportunities to express their views
- When necessary, deals effectively with power imbalances
- Moves parties from positions to interests
- Enables parties to vent their feelings
- Is sensitive to the dynamics between parties and between individuals in parties
- Enables parties to produce an agreement that is comprehensive, unambiguous and understood by all involved

Thinking Agility

The mediator demonstrates creative thinking and is able to see things in a different way. The mediator who has excellent thinking agility:

- Is able to keep one or more steps ahead of the parties
- Thinks "outside the box"
- Thinks laterally
- Listens to complex information and can then translate it into simple terms
- Can apply commercial solutions in a workplace setting
- Demonstrates ability to listen to and retain lots of information and quickly put into categories to help parties define priorities
- Is able to demonstrate ability to ask appropriate questions that will help parties think about potential solutions
- Demonstrates ability to change the environment or dynamics to break deadlock

Self Development

The mediator seeks opportunities to improve and develop personal skills and understanding of mediation. The mediator who is excellent in self-development:

- Keeps up to date with developments in mediation
- Analyses their own performance, where appropriate seeking feedback from observers, mentors and so on
- Is aware of their own areas of strength and development needs
- Actively seeks to address their own development needs
- Implements feedback from parties and/or mediation commissioners

Mediation Skills

The mediator's skill set will develop with experience. The skills of omni-partiality and impartiality are difficult skills to learn. We form judgements throughout our lives and become used to giving advice or giving points of view during dialogue. Working neutrally with others requires that we accept their perceptions and feelings, putting aside our own. In order to interact in a way that is genuine and responsive, we need to recognise the sources and extents of our own values and how they may affect our reaction to other people. A key quality for the mediator is to remain impartial and professionally detached without appearing aloof.

Mediators can become impatient if they can see a solution long before the parties do. It is essential, however, that the mediator allows the parties to reach a resolution at their own pace. Most experienced mediators will feel some apprehension before a mediation and exhilaration or disappointment at the end. It is important that, as mediator, you recognise and acknowledge that these feelings are part of our human nature.

The effective mediator:

- Should have an open mind
- Demonstrates a non-judgemental attitude, whilst helping the parties think about their position
- Does not pose a solution to the parties

Parties will build trust, almost immediately, in a mediator who demonstrates competence. This is done in the early stages by being able to competently describe the process and being able to empathise with the parties.

Research suggests that on first meeting the impact of how humans interact can be divided as:

- Words - 7%
- Tone of voice - 37%
- Body language – 56%

Communication Styles

The skill descriptors which follow below are intended to enable you to increase your awareness and your abilities to use such skills well.

Listening

The mediator needs to be able to understand a dispute from all sides. This means that the mediator must not only hear what a person is saying but also understand what they are saying and be able to see things from that person's point of view. To listen fully requires tremendous energy. Real listening takes us deeper and leads us to finding out new information.

Real listening means that we listen without thinking about our response to the speaker. We bring empathy and commitment to our listening by avoiding judgements and openly and honestly addressing what has brought the parties to the mediation table. When we listen fully, we are more likely to find out what lies beneath someone's angry words. The most subtle information lies beneath the surface of the communication. The deeper the listening, the greater the chances of hearing the subtleties. Listening is as much a part of communication as speaking.

Effective listening does not begin with listening, but with the listener clearing the decks and focusing his or her attention on the person who is about to speak. This means emptying your mind of all the thoughts competing for your attention – including what the other party has just said to you – and surrendering your ideas about what the speaker should not do or be. There is a crucial difference between hearing, which is physiological, and listening, which is psychological, between listening to people and listening with them.

Listening, like speaking, is largely a matter of intention. Its effectiveness depends on how important we think the information is to us. When we listen, we can listen only to the details of what someone is saying, but not to their deeper meaning.

Empathetic listening

When you listen with your heart, you become one with the speaker. Empathetic listening, for this reason, is much deeper than merely active or responsive listening. It requires you to focus your awareness not merely on the words being used but on what the speaker may be thinking or feeling without words. It means asking yourself what it might feel like to walk in your opponent's shoes, or what would cause you to make that statement or to communicate or behave as they did.

When you listen within a role - the way, for example, that a manager typically listens to an employee, a teacher listens to a student, or a government clerk listens to a member of the public - you are likely to be listening primarily to determine the facts or what you should do. You can also listen for subtle information about the speaker, how he or she perceives the world, and what is really important to them.

Thus, in addition to the facts, you can go deeper within yourself, access your empathy, and when listening to the parties, you may also be able to hear faint indications of, for example:

Emotions and feelings	Distortions of perception
Wishes and desires	Prejudices
Interests and positions	Family patterns
Dreams and visions	Role confusions
Intentions	Stereotypes
Humiliation	Self-esteem
Denials and defensiveness	Resistance
Openings to dialogue	Apologies
Similarities	Differences in style
Cries for help	Admissions of guilt
Desire for forgiveness	Acknowledgement

In truth, all of these elements are present in all our conversations, except that we generally do not really listen for them. As a mediator, you are more likely to get a successful resolution if you can hear these and other elements through what each party are saying.

Encouraging

Encouraging questions and comments and inviting speakers to share their feelings, perceptions, and attitudes. Comments such as "please tell me more,"

"I'm interested in what you are saying/thinking/feeling," "I would like to know your reactions," "I hear what you are saying", are inviting statements.

Clarifying

Ask questions that clarify the points being made by the speaker. Send a signal that you are interested in the speaker and the content of what is being said. Questions like "when did this happen?" "Who else was involved?" "What did it mean to you?" elicit detail and meaning. Clarifying questions de-escalate emotions by helping the speaker to focus on facts rather than feelings. Be careful not to interrogate the speaker with prying questions. Your tone of voice and intonation mark the difference between prying and clarifying.

Acknowledging

You can encourage greater openness by recognising, naming, and acknowledging the feelings being expressed. Comments like "I can see you are pretty upset about that. Can you tell me why?" or "I can appreciate why you might feel that way", give permission for greater depth of communication. Be careful not to assume you know what the other person is feeling. You can also use these expressions to give someone permission to say what they are feeling. Avoid popular catchphrases such as "it sounds like you are very angry right now" because they convey an impression that you are trying to manipulate the speaker and betray a lack of empathy rather than a presence of heart.

Soliciting

Ask questions to solicit advice and identify possible solutions, such as "Tell me more about what you want" "What would you like to happen?" "Why do you think that would work?" "What options do you see for settlement?" "Where would you like to go next?"

Mirroring

Mirroring reflects back the emotions, effect, demeanour, body language, tone of voice, metaphors, even breathing patterns used by the speaker as a way of encouraging the speaker to feel you are a companion in whatever he or she is thinking or feeling, rather than a dispassionate observer who does not really understand. If the speaker takes a defensive posture, you can try initially taking one yourself, then moving to a more open one. In doing so, do not make it appear that you are mimicking or being disrespectful.

Inviting elaboration

Asking open-ended questions that do not have a fixed answer lets the speaker know you want to hear his or her point of view. You can ask wide-open questions, such as "why?" "What would you like to see happen?" "Why is that important to you?" Or you can ask more direct questions, such as "I'd like to ask a question about that" or "how would you . . ." or "help me understand why you . . ." or "what might you ask that could get you the information?"

Responding
Listening respectfully also means responding authentically to what is said and not using listening techniques to manipulate the speaker. The speaker is entitled to a response that comes to terms with what was said. One approach is to say; "If I understand you correctly, you see the problem this way . . ." (summarise).

Summarising
If you want the other person to feel heard, summarise what was said in your own words, for example, by saying, "let me see if I understand what you just said . . . (summarise in your own words). Is that correct?" This feedback helps the speaker feel heard and provides an opportunity to confirm, correct, or improve your understanding of the other speaker's communications. It demonstrates your interest in what was said and your desire to grasp the essential meaning of the communication. It is useful to summarise at the end of a conversation to see if you have the same perception of what was said. In doing so, you risk making a mistake, but it is better to be mistaken and receive clarification than to continue based on a false assumption of what was meant.

Validating
Recognise the speaker's contribution and thank the person for communicating with you. Validate specific points the speaker made that you found useful in the conversation. You can make comments such as "I appreciate your willingness to raise these issues with me." "I learned a great deal from what you said, specifically . . ." "I know it took a lot for you to be open as you were, and I thank you for taking that risk." "I appreciate your willingness to talk to me about this."

Your challenge is to be as deeply honest and empathetic as you can; to become sincerely curious and interested in what each party is saying; to listen with your heart for other people's unspoken needs, interests, desires and intentions.

Questioning
For the mediator, questioning has two important purposes:

1.   To gather information and ensure that you understand that information

2.   To help parties think constructively about possible outcomes

- Open questions help to get people talking and open up new areas of discussion
- Closed questions help to focus people on particular facts

It is important that the mediator chooses the right type of question. To help with this skill, we can further categorise questions into four types:

TYPE	AIM IS TO	EXAMPLE
Exploring (Open)	Get information Open discussions Get explanations Broaden discussion	Who, what, where, when, why, how? What other issues should be considered?
Challenging (Open)	Challenges ideas and preconceptions Understand reasoning	What makes you say that?
Hypothetical (Open and Closed)	Develop new ideas Change course of discussion Unblock thinking	Suppose they did this, what would you do? What if....? Have you considered...?
Alternative (Closed)	Make decisions Select options	Which is preferable..? Will you do X or Y?

Here are some additional questions you can ask to promote open, ongoing, constructive dialogue in groups or organisations or with individuals.

We encourage you to invent your own:

- What are some of the grey areas in the position you have taken, or the areas you find difficult to define?

- Do the differences between your positions reveal any riddles, paradoxes, contradictions or enigmas about this issue? Is it possible to see your differences as two sides of the same coin? If so, what unites them? What is the coin?

- Can you separate the issue from the person with whom you are disagreeing? Is there anything positive you can say about the person on the other side of this issue?

- What processes or ground rules could help you disagree more constructively?

- Instead of focusing on the past, what would you like to see happen in the future? Why?

- Are you disagreeing over fundamental values or over how to achieve them?

- Is there a way both of you might be right? How?

- Would it be possible to test your ideas in practice and see which work best? How might you do that? What criteria could you use to decide what works best?

- What could be done to improve each idea? Could some of the other side's ideas be incorporated into yours?

- Are there any other alternatives to what you are both saying? Have you left anything out?

- How could you make dialogue ongoing? How can you preserve your differences so as not to lose sight of their truths?

- What could you do to improve your process for handling disagreements in the future? For encouraging future dialogue?

These questions contribute to a successful dialogue by enhancing the parties' engagement with the issues, each other and themselves, making it possible to interlace opposing ideas and interests. The role of mediators and facilitators is to initiate, model, encourage and improve the dialogue by deepening questions and building on answers.

Non-verbal communication
We can reveal our feelings and attitudes without saying a word. For example, a smile usually says "I'm happy", and looking at a watch may say "please get on with it". For the most part, non-verbal communication reveals emotions and feelings rather than giving information about the external world. It is easy to lie using words, but other aspects of communication make it less easy to deceive. For example, facial expressions are directly controlled by the emotional centres of the

brain and become hard to simulate. When you read the expression on another's face, you are more likely to assess the true emotion being felt than when you merely listen to what is being said.

As a mediator, your challenge is to not allow your expressions or body language to indicate how you might feel about what a party has said. For example, someone might say that "the fact that I was treated in this way really hurt me". You might feel that the person has a trivial point. It is important to keep an almost 'dead-pan' expression so as to not give away any of your personal feelings, as this will weaken or destroy your position as mediator.

Observation of parties' body language can also provide the mediator with important information. An open, relaxed posture can suggest that that is how they are feeling at that moment. Uncomfortable shifting in the chair, speech hesitations, stuttering and breathing changes can all suggest that the issue being dealt with is potentially distressing. Parties can also display other signs that indicate anxiety. These can include:

- Backward movement
- Tapping a hand on the leg
- Aggression
- Averting eyes
- Repeatedly touching the face

None of these behaviours are certainties, so should not be read in isolation. It is also important to note that many non-verbal signals are culturally relative – people from different cultures may well interpret some signals differently.

Problem solving and creativity
In order to add value, the mediator needs to feel able to engage in the process of problem solving with the parties. Initially, this may mean:

- *Defining the problem accurately* - the mediator will always try to define a problem in terms of outcome – that is, the place where you want to end up. This is because, having defined it, the mediator can then engage the parties in what is known technically as 'means-end analysis'. In means-end analysis the search for a solution begins at the outcome and works backwards to the present state (the means being the steps that must be taken to get from the present state - the problem - to the goal of solving the problem).

- *Clustering* - often, a dispute will consist of a number of different issues and the mediator may be able to help the parties to split these into separate categories (clustering) that can be resolved separately. The achievement of each cluster of issues can help the parties to get closer to achieving their overall goal.

Mediators often feel responsible for ensuring that the parties find a solution. It is tempting to suggest one that seems obvious, logical or expedient. Mediators, however, should remember that their role is to guide the parties to their own solution. Not only would a mediator's solution, if adopted, probably be less suitable than one the parties create themselves, it would also deprive the parties of the right and responsibility for determining their own future. Also, if the mediator's solution should fail, the parties could blame the mediator, rather than take responsibility themselves.

Experience has also shown that people have a higher commitment to a decision that they have generated for themselves. As long as the parties are progressing well on their own, the mediator should not intervene. The mediator can and should be prepared to intervene if the parties become stuck and appear to have run out of ideas.

Using a flip chart when clustering is invaluable. A flip chart allows all concerned to see what the issues are and helps crystallise the issues for discussion.

- *Creativity techniques that generate ideas for solutions* - the most popular creativity tool used in mediation is brainstorming. The strength of brainstorming lies in its simplicity - the only tools required are a flip chart and a marker pen. At the start of the session, the mediator clarifies the objective: for example, 'To produce ways in which this dispute may be resolved'. The mediator then ensures that everyone knows the rules of brainstorming, which are shown below, and sets a time limit (15 minutes is generally sufficient). The rules of brainstorming are:

  - Quantity rather than quality - the idea is to get as many ideas as possible. So be prepared to use lots of paper.

  - No criticism or judgement - this goes along with maximising numbers. All ideas should be written down. Any attempts to comment on them during the gathering stage should be politely silenced.

- Encourage freewheeling and build on others' ideas - one of the strengths of brain-storming is that it can 'spark off' ideas in other people. So encourage people to follow their trains of thought.

The mediator acts as scribe and must ensure that every idea is written down. During the brainstorming, the mediator may offer his or her own ideas, as long as she/he does not try to 'sell' those ideas to the parties. After the session the ideas are evaluated. The most promising ideas can be explored and expanded upon.

Other ways in which mediators can help ideas to start flowing include:

- *Summaries* - the mediator summarises the ideas mentioned so far, usually by writing them down. Seeing ideas in writing can sometimes prompt new ideas.

- *Using praise* - praising the parties for having made as much progress as they have can give them new impetus to solve problems.

- *Solution attribution* - analyse a solution by listing its attributes under two columns, '+' and '-'. Other ideas may come to mind during the process. Parties can also discuss ways of eliminating the items under the '-' column or try to find solutions that do not have these attributes.

- *Calling for a break* - too much focus on one issue can sometimes lead to "paralysis through analysis". By taking the spotlight off the issue, people's minds are sometimes unblocked (this phenomenon occurs when you have a problem to which a solution appears after you have 'slept on it').

- *Offering options* - this would appear to contradict the concept of the neutrality of the mediator. Yet provided that the mediator offers at least two solutions and does not try to sell them, then the responsibility remains with the parties as to whether they wish to pursue them or not.

- *BATNA and WATNA* - ask each side to develop their 'best alternative to a negotiated agreement' and their 'worst alternative to a negotiated agreement'. This will enable the parties to identify more precisely what is at stake in the dispute.

- *Stress the benefits of settlement* - re-iterate the parties' interests and needs and search for areas of flexibility. Stress the benefits of settlement in terms of future relationships or, where this is not appropriate, in terms of money saving, emotional turmoil, time and so on.

Concluding the Mediation

Every mediated settlement should be an agreement that:

- Satisfies the parties
- Deals with the issues in the dispute
- Is workable and practical
- Minimises or eliminates the possibility of any further dispute

Will it stick?
When a settlement agreement has been reached it is important that the mediator checks that all the points raised throughout the mediation have been covered and included in the settlement. There may also be some general points that would warrant being fed back to the organisation. These points shouldn't be specifically about the dispute, but rather about questioning whether the incident was a one-off or a signal of similar discord that might exist in other pockets of the organisation.

The settlement agreement
The settlement agreement should provide a record of the closing position of the mediation. It is important to capture this and ensure that it is agreed by both parties. If lawyers are present at the mediation, you should allow them to write any settlement agreement. As mediator you still have the responsibility to make sure that the agreement accurately reflects the agreed settlement position of both parties. This stage of the process can be difficult as everyone is tired and nerves may still be frayed. An agreement covering a range of complex issues can take a couple of hours, so the mediator's job is far from over. This part of the process needs the same attention as the mediation discussion.

The key points of any settlement agreement would cover areas such as:

- Identification of the parties
- Payment terms
- Working relationship arrangements
- Confidentiality
- Announcements/press
- Signatures

Other terms, such as ensuring that the mediator will not be called as a witness and the process being without prejudice, would usually be covered in the mediation agreement.

If settlement isn't reached, then remember that as mediator the problem doesn't become yours. The parties are always responsible. You should, however, attempt to make arrangements to keep dialogue going. Some mediations can settle the day after, as parties realise after a night's sleep that the main issues have surfaced and continuing the stand off would be futile. Globis Mediation Group recommends that you ask permission to maintain contact with the parties, meet the parties separately and agree a programme of action for next steps.

Clive Lewis

Conclusion

Assistant Mediators

You are most likely to begin developing your mediation career as an assistant mediator. This is an excellent opportunity to learn and develop your understanding of the mediation process. Take the time to review the experience with the lead mediator afterwards. Assess the strengths and skills that you bring to mediation and identify areas that require further work. As you progress, you may have an assistant mediator with you when you mediate. Assisting a mediator gives experience to those who have recently trained and it provides the mediator with a valuable companion. It is up to you as the mediator to agree on the assistant mediator's specific role. If you decide that you are to retain the lead throughout the mediation, allow your assistant to ask you questions to keep abreast with your train of thought.

An assistant mediator may have a specific role such as:

- A note taker to allow you to take the briefest of notes
- An observer to watch the body language of those involved in the conversation
- A runner for messages
- Someone who you bounce thoughts and ideas off – mediation can be lonely work if there is no one to share the pain and joy with you

After the mediation, an assistant can help you review the day, discuss what went well and what you could do differently.

Effective Mediators

The effective mediator will:

- Engage in valuable dialogue with the mediation commissioner
    - Take a thorough brief
    - Explain the mediation process

- Thoroughly explain the process and set the scene with the parties
    - Arrange the physical environment
    - Display confidence and understanding with the mediation process
    - Pay attention to parties' needs
    - Convey energy and enthusiasm

- Build rapport and trust with the parties
  - Mirror behaviours appropriately
  - Dress suitably
  - Use appropriate language
  - Use humour where suitable
  - Listen deeply and offer apt responses
  - Prepare thoroughly
  - Demonstrate omni-partiality at all times

- Keep the process moving
  - Keep the parties focused
  - Assess the right time to use the right method
  - Encourage the parties to think creatively
  - Move to unblock impasse
  - Maintain high energy levels
  - Summarise and check confidentialities before moving on
  - Work on options and avoid reaching premature conclusions
  - Manage time well

- Demonstrate competence throughout
  - Open the mediation well
  - Answer questions ably
  - Handle challenges confidently
  - Move smoothly from one interaction to another
  - Remain aware of commercial and other practical factors that need to be considered for a solution to be workable
  - Make the parties feel at ease

- Continue to learn and develop
  - Document learning from every mediation
  - Keep abreast of workplace mediation developments
  - Read leading articles and books on workplace mediation
  - Apply learning to new situations
  - Take responsibility for continuing professional development as a mediator

Some Do's and Don'ts for Effective Employment and Workplace Mediation

The points below serve as a reminder for highlighting and reinforcing guidelines and good practice.

The do's

- Prepare, prepare, prepare. Do your homework. It is critical that as mediator you know the facts to the case you are dealing with and have all key points at hand

- Learn from previous mediations and implement feedback with new situations

- Develop a suitable opening that demonstrates your competence and builds rapport and trust with the parties

- Remain neutral at all times. This will allow the mediation to keep flowing

- Acknowledge emotions and allow them to be vented

- Encourage all present to contribute to the proceedings and invite contributions from quieter participants

- Have patience – remember to let the parties own the problem as well as the solution

- Be willing to change your strategy if something isn't working

- Reality-check where necessary

- Be prepared to keep going through the tough times

- Mediation is hard work - get plenty of rest prior to and following the mediation

The don'ts
- Don't be tempted to take sides. Remember your position of neutrality (or omni-partiality)

- Don't get too involved in taking notes – remember to keep good eye contact with the parties

- Don't interrupt

- Don't make suggestions about options for resolution

- If you have adhered to the list of do's, don't take it personally if mediation fails

- Don't believe that parties aren't interested in settling their dispute – even if they say they aren't

- Don't believe that parties can't increase their 'bottom line' offer

Ethics and Standards

The role of the mediator is a privileged and sensitive one. The parties place considerable trust in the mediator. This particularly applies in relation to confidential and emotional information that is shared on the day. Mediators who do not display the highest standard of ethics are likely to find that their mediation career is short-lived.

Impartiality and neutrality are fundamental to the role of the mediator who must always remain impartial in relation to content, process and outcome of the mediation. This is particularly important for workplace mediations. For example, if trust is broken by an in-house mediator during a workplace mediation session, an organisation will struggle to give the mediation concept a good reputation and employees will lose faith in the process.

Summary

As an employment and workplace mediator you have the opportunity to make a tremendous difference. Although hard work, mediation can be a truly rewarding experience (in non-financial ways). As you develop your skills in this area, we encourage you to remember that through you, individuals and organisations can be released from their difficulties and are then free to focus on more positive things. Your skill as a mediator can create a life changing experience for someone and be the catalyst that allows them to wake up to living without the conflict that has proved so costly. Globis Mediation Group is here to help you as your mediation career develops. Please don't hesitate to be in touch for help, support or guidance should you need it.

Appendix 1

Overview of Globis Mediation Group

About Globis Mediation Group

Globis Mediation Group specialises in building better relationships at work and is widely regarded as one of the best practice workplace mediation providers in the UK. Having secured numerous public and private sector clients, Globis Mediation Group will continue to set the pace for growth in this sector.

In 2011, Globis Mediation Group achieved 90.7% successful outcomes from workplace mediations, including individual, team and corporate disputes. Globis Mediation Group's service includes advising organisations on methods they can adopt to prevent future escalation of conflict. Globis provides world class in-house and public accredited mediation training. In addition:

- Globis Mediation Group is one of the UK's leading providers of preventative and remedial solutions that help organisations build better relationships at work.

- Every year hundreds of people are trained by Globis Mediation Group to become accredited workplace mediators.

- Globis Mediation Group works in both the public and private sectors.

- In 2007, Globis Mediation Group advised the Department for Business on the development of the Gibbons Review which led to the repeal of the statutory dispute procedures. Globis Mediation Group also advised the CIPD on their response to the review.

- Globis Mediation Group is a board member of the Civil Mediation Council and the National Certificate in Workplace and Employment Mediation is accredited by the Law Society, Bar Standards Council and apt awards.

- Globis Mediation Group recently helped East Sussex County Council save almost £1 million in just one year by training an in-house mediation team. This scheme has won an award from the Public Sector People Managers Association.

- Most of Globis Mediation Group's work comes from referrals from current clients.

- Director of Globis Mediation Group, Clive Lewis, is the author of ten books covering the topics of workplace mediation, difficult conversations, performance management, redundancy and work-life balance.

- Clive was the Honorary Secretary of the Civil Mediation Council's Workplace Committee until 2012.

- He was awarded the OBE for Public Service in the Queen's Birthday Honours List of 2011, and appointed as Deputy Lieutenant of Gloucestershire in 2012.

Appendix 2

Mediation Procedure

Globis Mediation Group mediations shall be governed by the following procedure ("the Mediation Procedure"), as amended by Globis Mediation Group from time to time and the parties shall be taken to have agreed that the mediation shall be conducted in accordance with the Mediation Procedure.

1.   Mediation Procedure

1.1   The parties to a dispute or negotiation in question will attempt to settle it by mediation. Representatives of the parties, including their advisors (legal representatives) and the mediator, will attend the mediation sessions. Any and all communications relating to, and at, the mediation are private and confidential and will be without prejudice.

1.2   The representatives of the parties must have the necessary authority to settle the dispute. If a party is a natural person, that person must attend the mediation session. If a party is not a natural person it must be represented at the mediation session by an officer or employee with full authority to make binding agreements settling the dispute. If that person comes with "limited" authority - that is authority up to a certain amount - he or she must disclose this information to the mediator prior to the mediation.

1.3   The procedure at the mediation will be determined by the mediator.

1.4   The parties will agree to the appointment of a Globis Mediation Group accredited mediator. Globis Mediation Group will provide to the parties, in advance of the mediation, details of recommended mediators drawn from the Globis Mediation Group panel of mediators. If the parties are unable to agree to the appointment of a mediator, Globis Mediation Group will appoint a mediator if requested to do so.

2.   Mediation Agreement

2.1   The parties and Globis Mediation Group will enter into and sign an agreement ("Agreement to Mediate") in advance of the mediation and this agreement shall govern the relationship between the parties before, during and after the mediation.

2.2   Each party, in signing the Agreement to Mediate, will be deemed to be agreeing on behalf of both itself and all such other persons, to be bound by the confidentiality provisions of the Mediation Procedure.

3.   The Mediator

3.1   The mediator will:

     3.1.1   Attend any meetings with any or all of the parties preceding the mediation if requested to do so, or if the mediator decides it is appropriate;

     3.1.2   Prior to the commencement of the mediation, read and familiarise himself/herself with each party's position statement and any documents provided in accordance with paragraph 6.1 below;

     3.1.3   Determine the procedure (see paragraph 1.3 above);

     3.1.4   Assist the parties in drawing up any written settlement agreement;

     3.1.5   Abide by the terms of the Mediation Procedure, the Agreement to Mediate and the Globis Mediation Group Code of Practice (as amended from time to time) ("Code of Practice").

3.2   The mediator will not:

     3.2.1   Impose a settlement on the parties;
     3.2.2   Offer legal advice or act as legal advisor to any party;
     3.2.3   Analyse a party's legal position or rights.

4.   Mediation Arrangements

Globis Mediation Group will, in consultation with the parties and the mediator, make the necessary arrangements for the mediation including, as appropriate:

4.1   Recommending mediators with regard to, inter alia, the nature of the dispute, degree of complexity, location of parties etc and drawing up the Agreement to Mediate;

4.2   Liaising between the parties to agree suitable date and venue;

4.3 Assisting the parties in preparing their position statement (see paragraph 6) and supporting documentation;

4.4 Discussing or meeting with any or all of the parties or their representatives (and the mediator, if appropriate), either together or separately, on any matter prior to the proposed mediation;

4.5 General administration in relation to the mediation.

5. Representation
5.1 Parties do not require legal representation to attend the mediation.

5.2 Where a party is un-represented, Globis Mediation Group encourages such party to obtain independent legal advice prior to the mediation.

5.3 Each party is required to notify Globis Mediation Group and other parties involved in the mediation of the names of those people intended to be present on its behalf at the mediation.

6. Position Statements & Documentation
6.1 Each party will be required to prepare and deliver to the mediator, within seven (7) days of the mediation, a concise summary ("Position Statement") of the case in dispute and copies of any and all documents referred to in the position statement and which it will be seeking to refer to during the mediation.

6.2 Globis Mediation Group does not impose any obligation on the parties to exchange position statements, but parties are free to agree to the simultaneous exchange of the position statements, if so agreed or if considered appropriate.

6.3 The position statement is private and confidential and will not be disclosed (by the mediator) to any other third party unless expressly authorised to do so.

6.4 Parties are encouraged to prepare and agree a joint bundle of documents where appropriate.

7. The Mediation
7.1 No formal record or transcript of the mediation will be made.

7.2   The mediation session is for the purpose of attempting to achieve a negotiated settlement and all information provided during the mediation session is without prejudice and will be inadmissible in any tribunal proceedings or litigation of the dispute.

7.3   If the parties are unable to reach a settlement during the mediation, the mediator may, if requested to do so, facilitate further negotiation after the mediation session itself has ended.

8.   Settlement Agreement

Any settlement reached in the mediation will not be legally binding until it has been recorded in writing and signed by, or on behalf of, the parties.

9.   Termination

Any of the parties may withdraw from the mediation at any time and shall immediately inform the mediator and the other representatives either orally or in writing. The mediation will terminate when:

9.1   A party voluntarily withdraws from the mediation; or
9.2   A written settlement agreement is concluded; or
9.3   The mediator elects, in his/her sole discretion, that continuing the mediation is unlikely to result in a settlement.

10.   Effect on Legal Proceedings

Where the dispute has been referred to mediation by a tribunal, or where a tribunal has ordered that the parties consider mediation and the mediation does not achieve settlement, the current litigation in relation to the dispute may be commenced or continued, notwithstanding the mediation, unless the parties agree otherwise.

11.   Confidentiality

11.1   Every person involved in the mediation will keep confidential and not use for any collateral or ulterior purpose:

11.1.1   The fact that the mediation is to take place or has taken place;

11.1.2   All information, (whether given orally or in writing or otherwise), produced for, or arising pursuant to, the mediation including the settlement agreement (if any) arising out of it except insofar as is necessary to implement and enforce any such settlement agreement.

11.2 All documents (which include anything upon which evidence is recorded, including tapes or computer discs) or other information produced for, or arising in relation to, the mediation will be privileged and not admissible as evidence or discoverable in any tribunal proceedings or litigation connected with the dispute.

11.3 The parties will not subpoena or otherwise require the mediator, Globis Mediation Group (or any employee, consultant, director or representative of Globis Mediation Group) or any other person attending the mediation under the auspices of Globis Mediation Group to testify or produce records, notes or any other information or material whatsoever in any future or continuing proceedings.

12. Mediation Costs

12.1 It is usual that the costs of the mediation are borne equally between the parties in employment mediation cases.

12.2 It is usual that the costs of the mediation are borne by the organisation in workplace mediation cases.

12.3 Payment of costs for the mediation will be made to Globis Ltd .

12.4 Each party attending the mediation is to bear its own costs and expenses of its participation in the mediation (including legal representative costs) unless agreed otherwise.

13. Waiver of Liability

Neither the mediator nor Globis Mediation Group shall be liable to the parties for any act or omission in connection with the services provided by them in, or in relation to, the mediation, unless the act or omission is fraudulent or involves wilful misconduct.

14. Human Rights

The referral of a dispute to mediation does not affect any rights that may exist under Article 6 of the European Convention of Human Rights. Should the dispute not settle through the process of mediation, the parties' right to go to tribunal or pursue a court trial shall remain unaffected.

Appendix 3

Code of Practice

All Globis Mediation Group accredited mediators subscribe to the European code of practice ("Code of Practice") for employment and workplace mediation. Globis Mediation Group recommends that all mediators who offer Globis Mediation Group services (including mediation) comply with a code of practice.

1.   Qualifications and Appointment of a Mediator

1.1   Every mediator must comply with the criteria and requirements for mediators stipulated from time to time by Globis Mediation Group, including those relating to training, consultancy, accreditation and regulation.

1.2   A mediator may only accept an appointment to mediate if both or all the parties to the mediation so request or agree.

1.3   A mediator may only continue to act as such so long as both or all parties to the mediation wish him or her to do so. If any party does not wish to continue with the mediation, the mediator must discontinue the process. Also, if the mediator considers that it would be inappropriate to continue the mediation, the mediator shall bring it to an end, and may, subject to the terms of the mediation agreement, decline to give reasons.

2.   Conflicts of Interest, Confidential Information and the Impartiality of the Mediator

2.1   The impartiality of mediators is a fundamental principle of mediation.

2.2   Impartiality means that:

2.2.1   the mediator does not have any significant personal interest in the outcome of the mediation;

2.2.2   the mediator will conduct the process fairly and even-handedly, and will not favour any party over another

2.3   Save as set out in 2.2 above, a mediator with an insignificant interest in the personal outcome of the mediation may act, if full disclosure is made to all of the parties as soon as it is known, and they consent.

2.4   The mediator must not act, or, if having started to do so, continue to act if any circumstances exist which may constitute an actual or potential conflict of interest.

3.   Mediation Procedures

3.1   The mediator must ensure that the parties agree the terms and conditions regulating the mediation before dealing with the substantive issues. This should be in a written agreement which should reflect the main principles of this code.

3.2   The procedure for the conduct of the mediation is a matter for the decision of the mediator. Insofar as the mediator establishes an agenda of matters to be covered in the mediation, the mediator shall be guided by the needs, wishes and priorities of the parties in doing so.

3.3   In establishing any procedures for the conduct of the mediation, the mediator must be guided by a commitment to procedural fairness and a high quality of process.

4.   The Decision Making Process

4.1   The primary aim of the mediation is to help the parties to arrive at their own decisions regarding the disputed issues.

4.2   The parties should be helped to reach such resolution of such issues which they feel are appropriate to their particular circumstances. Such resolution may not necessarily be the same as that which may be arrived at in a tribunal. That allows the parties to explore and agree upon a wider range of options for settlement that might otherwise be the case.

4.3   The mediator may meet the parties individually and/or together. Solicitors, barristers or other professional advisors acting for the individual parties may, but need not necessarily, participate in the mediation process if the parties so wish. Such solicitors and/or advisors may take part in discussions and meetings, with or without the parties, and in other communication and representation, in such manner as the mediator may consider useful and appropriate.

4.4   Parties are free to consult with the individual professional advisors as the mediation progresses. The mediator may make suggestions to the parties as to the appropriateness of seeking further assistance from professional advisors such as lawyers, accountants, expert valuers or others.

4.5   The mediator must not seek to impose his or her preferred outcome on the parties.

4.6   The mediator shall be free to make management decisions with regard to the conduct of the mediation process.

4.7   The mediator may suggest possible solutions and help the parties to explore these, where he or she thinks this would be helpful to them.

4.8   The mediator must recognise that the parties can reach decisions on any issues at any stage of the mediation.

4.9   At the end of the mediation or at any interim stage, the mediator and/or the parties or their representatives may prepare a written memorandum or summary of any agreements reached by the parties.

4.10   If the parties wish to consult their respective individual legal advisors before entering into any binding agreement, then any terms which they may provisionally propose as the basis for resolution will not be binding on them until they have each had the opportunity of taking advice from such legal advisors and have thereafter agreed, in writing, to be bound.

4.11   The mediator may assist the parties, so far as appropriate and practicable, to identify what information and documents will help the resolution of any issue(s), and how best such information and documents should be obtained. However, the mediator has no obligation to make independent enquiries or undertake verification in relation to any information or documents sought or provided in the mediation.

4.12   If, in cases where one or more parties is unrepresented at the mediation and the parties are proposing a resolution which appears to the mediator to be unworkable, having regard to the circumstances, then the mediator must inform the parties accordingly and may terminate the mediation and/or refer the parties to their legal advisors.

5.   Dealing with Power Imbalances

5.1   The mediator should be aware of power imbalances existing between the parties. If such imbalances seem likely to cause the mediation process to become unfair or ineffective, the mediator must take reasonable steps to try to prevent this.

5.2   The mediator must seek, in particular, to prevent abusive or intimidating behaviour by any of the parties.

5.3   If the mediator believes that, because of power imbalances, the mediation would not be able to be fairly and effectively conducted, he or she may discuss this with the parties, recognising that the mediation may have been brought to an end and/or the parties referred to their lawyers.

6.   Confidentiality and Privilege

6.1   Before the mediation commences, the parties should agree in writing as to the provisions concerning confidentiality and privilege that will apply to the mediation process itself and any resultant mediation agreement, save as otherwise agreed in the mediation settlement agreement.

6.2   The mediator must maintain confidentiality in relation to all matters dealt with in the mediation. The mediator may disclose:

6.2.1   matters which the parties and the mediator agree may be disclosed;

6.2.2   matters which are already public;

6.2.3   matters which the mediator considers appropriate where he or she believes that if the life or safety of any person is or may be at serious risk;

6.2.4   matters where the law imposes an overriding obligation of disclosure on the mediator.

6.3   Subject to paragraph 6.2 above, where the mediator meets the parties separately and obtains information from any party which is confidential to that party, the mediator must maintain the confidentiality of that information from all other parties, except to the extent that the mediator has been authorised to disclose any such information.

6.4   Mediators should note that the mediation privilege will not ordinarily apply in relation to communications indicating that a person is suffering or likely to suffer serious bodily harm, or where other public policy considerations prevail, or where for any other reason, the rules of evidence render privilege inapplicable.

6.5   The mediator should remind the parties that (unless the mediation agreement provides otherwise) the confidentiality and privilege attaching to the mediation process may not extend to the provisions of any settlement agreement which results. The mediator should suggest to the parties that they consider the extent to which they wish the terms of the resulting settlement to be disclosed – and to provide accordingly in the agreement itself.

7. Professional Indemnity Cover

All mediators should carry professional indemnity cover in respect of their acting as mediators outside their own organisation.

Clive Lewis

Appendix 4

Terms and Conditions of Business

Liability for the mediation fees

1. Unless agreement is reached to the contrary, the mediation fee, together with any other expenses, will be borne equally between the parties or by the organisation in the event of a workplace mediation.

2. Responsibility for fees rests with the mediating commissioner or instructing solicitor. In employment mediation cases Globis Mediation Group recommends that the instructing solicitors retain sufficient money on account to cover the mediation fee.

Cancellation policy

3. In certain instances, postponement of a mediation is inevitable. No cancellation fee will apply to a postponed mediation, other than to any irrecoverable expenses (e.g. venue cancellation fees). Globis Mediation Group will charge the following fees if the mediation is cancelled:

    3.1 more than 15 working days before the mediation was due to take place, 50% of the mediation fee shall be payable and any irrecoverable expenses (such as venue costs etc) incurred;

    3.2 between six and 14 days before the mediation was due to take place, 75% of the mediation fee and any additional irrecoverable expenses incurred will be payable.

    3.3 less than 6 working days before the mediation was due to take place, the full fee and any additional irrecoverable expenses incurred will be payable.

Appendix 5

Agreement to Mediate

THE FOLLOWING PARTIES namely:

A.   ....

B.   ....

(collectively the "Parties") hereby agree to mediate their dispute on the following terms and conditions:

1.   MEDIATION PROCEDURES

1.1   The mediation shall be held and conducted according to this Agreement to Mediate ("Mediation Agreement").

1.2   Parties will attend the mediation personally.

1.3   Any settlement reached in the mediation will not be binding until it has been reduced to writing and signed by each of the Parties ("settlement agreement").

2.   MEDIATOR

2.1   The parties agree that .... appointed by Globis Mediation Group Ltd will be the mediator.

2.2   The parties and the mediator recognise that the mediator is both impartial and neutral.

2.3   The parties recognise that the mediator does not offer legal advice or act as a legal advisor for any of the parties of the mediation nor will they provide any party with a legal analysis to protect any party's legal position or rights.

3. PLACE AND TIME OF THE MEDIATION

The mediation will take place at ………… on ………… starting at …………
am/pm.

4. MEDIATION FEES, EXPENSES AND COSTS

The mediator's fees and any other expenses associated with the
mediation will be shared equally between the parties [or borne by the
organisation].

5. PRIVATE SESSIONS

Information gained by the mediator through such a session is
confidential unless (a) it is in any event publicly available or (b) the
mediator is specifically authorised by that party to disclose it. This clause
is subject to Clause 6.

6. CONFIDENTIALITY

6.1 The mediator and the parties undertake to one another that they will
maintain confidentiality in respect of all statements and matters arising
in the mediation. The confidentiality provisions in this agreement are,
however, subject to the following exceptions:

6.1.1 Confidentiality does not apply insofar as any party needs to
disclose any such statements and matters in order to comply
with any statutory obligation or obtain professional advice.

6.1.2 Without prejudice to the generality of the above, the mediator
has an absolute obligation under the Proceeds of Crime Act
2002 to report to the National Crime Intelligence Service any
knowledge or suspicion relating to the involvement of the
proceeds of crime (including tax evasion) and is precluded by
law from informing the parties of his intention to do so.

6.2 The parties recognise that the mediation is for the purpose of attempting
to achieve a workable solution or negotiated settlement and as such all
information provided during the mediation is without prejudice and will
be inadmissible in any litigation or arbitration of the dispute.

6.3   The parties will not subpoena the mediator in any future or continuing proceedings.

7.   TERMINATION OF THE MEDIATION

Any of the parties or the mediator shall be entitled, in their absolute discretion, to terminate the mediation at any time without giving a reason.

8.   HUMAN RIGHTS

The referral of this dispute to mediation does not affect the rights that may exist under Article 6 of the European Convention on Human Rights.

9.   SIGNATURE OF THIS MEDIATION AGREEMENT

This Mediation Agreement is to be signed by each party.

A.

Signed: _____

Name: _____

B.

Signed: _____

Name: _____

C.

Signed: _____ (The Mediator)

Name: _____

Date: _____

Appendix 6

Recommended Reading

1. **The Mind Map Book**
   Buzan T (2000 revised ed.) - BBC Consumer Publishing (ISBN 0563537329)

2. **People Watching**
   Coleman V (1995) - Blue Books (ISBN 1899726004)

3. **Heart of the Mind**
   Connirae A & Andreas S (1989) - Real People Press (ISBN 0911226311)

4. **Everyone Can Win: How to Resolve Conflict**
   Cornelius H & Faire S (1995) - East Roseville, NSW: Simon & Schuster
   (ISBN 0713861113)

5. **Business Mediation: What You Need to Know**
   Coulson R (1987) - American Arbitration Association (ISBN 0943001072)

6. **The 7 Habits of Highly Effective People**
   Covey S (1999) - Simon & Schuster (ISBN 0684858398)

7. **The 8th Habit**
   Covey S (2004) - Simon & Schuster (ISBN 0743206827)

8. **Resolving Conflicts at Work**
   Cloke K (2005) - (ISBN 0787980242)

9. **Constructive Conflict Management**
   Crawley J (1992) - Nicholas Brealey Publishing (ISBN 1857880145)

10. **The Magic of Conflict**
    Crum T (1999) - Pocket Books (ISBN 0684854481)

11. **Skills for the Future**
    Dilts R & Bonissone G (1993) - Meta Publications (ISBN 0916990273)

12. **Getting to Yes**
    Fisher R & Ury W (1997) - Arrow (ISBN 0099248425)

13. **Social Skills at Work**
    Fontana D (1990) - Routeledge / British Psychological Society
    (ISBN 1854330152)

14. **Emotional Intelligence**
    Goleman D (1996) - Bloomsbury (ISBN 0747528306)

15. **Working With Emotional Intelligence**
    Goleman D (1999) - Bloomsbury (ISBN 0747543844)

16. **Piloting Through Chaos**
    Gresser J (1996) - Five Rings Press (ISBN 1888278005)

17. **Planning Under Pressure**
    Hickling A & Friend J (1997) - Butterworth & Heineman (ISBN 075062955)

18. **The Manager as Negotiator**
    Lax D A & Sebenius J K (1986) - Free Press (ISBN 0029187702)

19. **Curing Conflict**
    Lewis Leslie P (1994) – Pitman (ISBN 0207360559)

20. **Mediation in Context**
    Liebmann M (2000) - Jessica Kingsley Publishers (ISBN 1853026182)

21. **Introducing Neuro-Linguistic Programming**
    O'Connor J & Seymour J (2000) - Thorsons (ISBN 1855383446)

22. **Difficult Conversations**
    Stone D Patton B & Heen S (2000) - Penguin (ISBN 014027782X)

23. **Good to Great**
    Collins J (2001) - Random House (ISBN 0712676090)

24. **How the Mighty Fall**
    Collins J (2009) – Random House (ISBN 0977326411)

25. **Win Win: Resolving Workplace Conflict: 12 Stories**
    Lewis C (2011) – Roper Penberthy (ISBN 1903905702)

26. **The Definitive Guide to Workplace Mediation & Managing Conflict at Work**
Lewis C (2009) – Roper Penberthy (ISBN 9781903905364)

27. **Difficult Conversations: 10 Steps to Becoming a Tackler not a Dodger**
Lewis C (2011) – Bell & Bain (ISBN 9780956864802)

28. **Performance Management: 10 Steps to Getting the Most from Your Workforce**
Lewis C (2012) – Berforts Information Press (ISBN 9780956864888)

29. **Difficult Conversations in Dementia: A Ten Step Toolkit for Clinicians Involved in End of Life Discussions**
Lewis C (2012) – Berforts Information Press (ISBN 9780956864895)

30. **Work-Life Balance: How to Put Work in its Place and Reclaim Your Life**
Lewis C (2012) – Good News Digital Books (ISBN 9780956864864)

31. **Bouncing Back From Redundancy: 12 Steps to Get Your Career and Life Back on Track**
Lewis C (2011) – Good News Digital Books (ISBN 9780956864857)

32. **Looking for Your Next Job? Work: Where to Find it and How to Get Hired**
Lewis C (2014) – Berforts Information Press (ISBN 978095724613)

33. **Leadership with Compassion: Applying Kindness, Dignity and Respect in Healthcare Management**
Lewis C (2013) – Berforts Information Press (ISBN 9780957524606)

<u>Notes</u>